FREE Test Taking Tips Video/DVD Offer

To better serve you, we created videos covering test taking tips that we want to give you for FREE. **These videos cover world-class tips that will help you succeed on your test.**

We just ask that you send us feedback about this product. Please let us know what you thought about it—whether good, bad, or indifferent.

To get your **FREE videos**, you can use the QR code below or email freevideos@studyguideteam.com with "Free Videos" in the subject line and the following information in the body of the email:

    a. The title of your product

    b. Your product rating on a scale of 1-5, with 5 being the highest

    c. Your feedback about the product

If you have any questions or concerns, please don't hesitate to contact us at info@studyguideteam.com.

Thank you!

RICA Prep Book

Study Guide with Practice Tests
(Updated for the Revised Exam Outline)
[5th Edition]

Joshua Rueda

Interested in buying more than 10 copies of our product? Contact us about bulk discounts:
bulkorders@studyguideteam.com

ISBN 13: 9781637756959
ISBN 10: 163775695X

Table of Contents

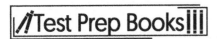

Welcome

Dear Reader,

Welcome to your new Test Prep Books study guide! We are pleased that you chose us to help you prepare for your exam. There are many study options to choose from, and we appreciate you choosing us. Studying can be a daunting task, but we have designed a smart, effective study guide to help prepare you for what lies ahead.

Whether you're a parent helping your child learn and grow, a high school student working hard to get into your dream college, or a nursing student studying for a complex exam, we want to help give you the tools you need to succeed. We hope this study guide gives you the skills and the confidence to thrive, and we can't thank you enough for allowing us to be part of your journey.

In an effort to continue to improve our products, we welcome feedback from our customers. We look forward to hearing from you. Suggestions, success stories, and criticisms can all be communicated by emailing us at info@studyguideteam.com.

Sincerely,
Test Prep Books Team

FREE Videos/DVD OFFER

Doing well on your exam requires both knowing the test content and understanding how to use that knowledge to do well on the test. We offer completely FREE test taking tip videos. **These videos cover world-class tips that you can use to succeed on your test.**

To get your **FREE videos**, you can use the QR code below or email freevideos@studyguideteam.com with "Free Videos" in the subject line and the following information in the body of the email:

   a. The title of your product
   b. Your product rating on a scale of 1-5, with 5 being the highest
   c. Your feedback about the product

If you have any questions or concerns, please don't hesitate to contact us at info@studyguideteam.com.

Quick Overview

As you draw closer to taking your exam, effective preparation becomes more and more important. Thankfully, you have this study guide to help you get ready. Use this guide to help keep your studying on track and refer to it often.

This study guide contains several key sections that will help you be successful on your exam. The guide contains tips for what you should do the night before and the day of the test. Also included are test-taking tips. Knowing the right information is not always enough. Many well-prepared test takers struggle with exams. These tips will help equip you to accurately read, assess, and answer test questions.

A large part of the guide is devoted to showing you what content to expect on the exam and to helping you better understand that content. In this guide are practice test questions so that you can see how well you have grasped the content. Then, answer explanations are provided so that you can understand why you missed certain questions.

Don't try to cram the night before you take your exam. This is not a wise strategy for a few reasons. First, your retention of the information will be low. Your time would be better used by reviewing information you already know rather than trying to learn a lot of new information. Second, you will likely become stressed as you try to gain a large amount of knowledge in a short amount of time. Third, you will be depriving yourself of sleep. So be sure to go to bed at a reasonable time the night before. Being well-rested helps you focus and remain calm.

Be sure to eat a substantial breakfast the morning of the exam. If you are taking the exam in the afternoon, be sure to have a good lunch as well. Being hungry is distracting and can make it difficult to focus. You have hopefully spent lots of time preparing for the exam. Don't let an empty stomach get in the way of success!

When travelling to the testing center, leave earlier than needed. That way, you have a buffer in case you experience any delays. This will help you remain calm and will keep you from missing your appointment time at the testing center.

Be sure to pace yourself during the exam. Don't try to rush through the exam. There is no need to risk performing poorly on the exam just so you can leave the testing center early. Allow yourself to use all of the allotted time if needed.

Remain positive while taking the exam even if you feel like you are performing poorly. Thinking about the content you should have mastered will not help you perform better on the exam.

Once the exam is complete, take some time to relax. Even if you feel that you need to take the exam again, you will be well served by some down time before you begin studying again. It's often easier to convince yourself to study if you know that it will come with a reward!

Test-Taking Strategies

1. Predicting the Answer

When you feel confident in your preparation for a multiple-choice test, try predicting the answer before reading the answer choices. This is especially useful on questions that test objective factual knowledge. By predicting the answer before reading the available choices, you eliminate the possibility that you will be distracted or led astray by an incorrect answer choice. You will feel more confident in your selection if you read the question, predict the answer, and then find your prediction among the answer choices. After using this strategy, be sure to still read all of the answer choices carefully and completely. If you feel unprepared, you should not attempt to predict the answers. This would be a waste of time and an opportunity for your mind to wander in the wrong direction.

2. Reading the Whole Question

Too often, test takers scan a multiple-choice question, recognize a few familiar words, and immediately jump to the answer choices. Test authors are aware of this common impatience, and they will sometimes prey upon it. For instance, a test author might subtly turn the question into a negative, or he or she might redirect the focus of the question right at the end. The only way to avoid falling into these traps is to read the entirety of the question carefully before reading the answer choices.

3. Looking for Wrong Answers

Long and complicated multiple-choice questions can be intimidating. One way to simplify a difficult multiple-choice question is to eliminate all of the answer choices that are clearly wrong. In most sets of answers, there will be at least one selection that can be dismissed right away. If the test is administered on paper, the test taker could draw a line through it to indicate that it may be ignored; otherwise, the test taker will have to perform this operation mentally or on scratch paper. In either case, once the obviously incorrect answers have been eliminated, the remaining choices may be considered. Sometimes identifying the clearly wrong answers will give the test taker some information about the correct answer. For instance, if one of the remaining answer choices is a direct opposite of one of the eliminated answer choices, it may well be the correct answer. The opposite of obviously wrong is obviously right! Of course, this is not always the case. Some answers are obviously incorrect simply because they are irrelevant to the question being asked. Still, identifying and eliminating some incorrect answer choices is a good way to simplify a multiple-choice question.

4. Don't Overanalyze

Anxious test takers often overanalyze questions. When you are nervous, your brain will often run wild, causing you to make associations and discover clues that don't actually exist. If you feel that this may be a problem for you, do whatever you can to slow down during the test. Try taking a deep breath or counting to ten. As you read and consider the question, restrict yourself to the particular words used by the author. Avoid thought tangents about what the author *really* meant, or what he or she was *trying* to say. The only things that matter on a multiple-choice test are the words that are actually in the question. You must avoid reading too much into a multiple-choice question, or supposing that the writer meant something other than what he or she wrote.

3

5. No Need for Panic

It is wise to learn as many strategies as possible before taking a multiple-choice test, but it is likely that you will come across a few questions for which you simply don't know the answer. In this situation, avoid panicking. Because most multiple-choice tests include dozens of questions, the relative value of a single wrong answer is small. As much as possible, you should compartmentalize each question on a multiple-choice test. In other words, you should not allow your feelings about one question to affect your success on the others. When you find a question that you either don't understand or don't know how to answer, just take a deep breath and do your best. Read the entire question slowly and carefully. Try rephrasing the question a couple of different ways. Then, read all of the answer choices carefully. After eliminating obviously wrong answers, make a selection and move on to the next question.

6. Confusing Answer Choices

When working on a difficult multiple-choice question, there may be a tendency to focus on the answer choices that are the easiest to understand. Many people, whether consciously or not, gravitate to the answer choices that require the least concentration, knowledge, and memory. This is a mistake. When you come across an answer choice that is confusing, you should give it extra attention. A question might be confusing because you do not know the subject matter to which it refers. If this is the case, don't eliminate the answer before you have affirmatively settled on another. When you come across an answer choice of this type, set it aside as you look at the remaining choices. If you can confidently assert that one of the other choices is correct, you can leave the confusing answer aside. Otherwise, you will need to take a moment to try to better understand the confusing answer choice. Rephrasing is one way to tease out the sense of a confusing answer choice.

7. Your First Instinct

Many people struggle with multiple-choice tests because they overthink the questions. If you have studied sufficiently for the test, you should be prepared to trust your first instinct once you have carefully and completely read the question and all of the answer choices. There is a great deal of research suggesting that the mind can come to the correct conclusion very quickly once it has obtained all of the relevant information. At times, it may seem to you as if your intuition is working faster even than your reasoning mind. This may in fact be true. The knowledge you obtain while studying may be retrieved from your subconscious before you have a chance to work out the associations that support it. Verify your instinct by working out the reasons that it should be trusted.

8. Key Words

Many test takers struggle with multiple-choice questions because they have poor reading comprehension skills. Quickly reading and understanding a multiple-choice question requires a mixture of skill and experience. To help with this, try jotting down a few key words and phrases on a piece of scrap paper. Doing this concentrates the process of reading and forces the mind to weigh the relative importance of the question's parts. In selecting words and phrases to write down, the test taker thinks about the question more deeply and carefully. This is especially true for multiple-choice questions that are preceded by a long prompt.

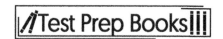

9. Subtle Negatives

One of the oldest tricks in the multiple-choice test writer's book is to subtly reverse the meaning of a question with a word like *not* or *except*. If you are not paying attention to each word in the question, you can easily be led astray by this trick. For instance, a common question format is, "Which of the following is...?" Obviously, if the question instead is, "Which of the following is not...?," then the answer will be quite different. Even worse, the test makers are aware of the potential for this mistake and will include one answer choice that would be correct if the question were not negated or reversed. A test taker who misses the reversal will find what he or she believes to be a correct answer and will be so confident that he or she will fail to reread the question and discover the original error. The only way to avoid this is to practice a wide variety of multiple-choice questions and to pay close attention to each and every word.

10. Reading Every Answer Choice

It may seem obvious, but you should always read every one of the answer choices! Too many test takers fall into the habit of scanning the question and assuming that they understand the question because they recognize a few key words. From there, they pick the first answer choice that answers the question they believe they have read. Test takers who read all of the answer choices might discover that one of the latter answer choices is actually *more* correct. Moreover, reading all of the answer choices can remind you of facts related to the question that can help you arrive at the correct answer. Sometimes, a misstatement or incorrect detail in one of the latter answer choices will trigger your memory of the subject and will enable you to find the right answer. Failing to read all of the answer choices is like not reading all of the items on a restaurant menu: you might miss out on the perfect choice.

11. Spot the Hedges

One of the keys to success on multiple-choice tests is paying close attention to every word. This is never truer than with words like almost, most, some, and sometimes. These words are called "hedges" because they indicate that a statement is not totally true or not true in every place and time. An absolute statement will contain no hedges, but in many subjects, the answers are not always straightforward or absolute. There are always exceptions to the rules in these subjects. For this reason, you should favor those multiple-choice questions that contain hedging language. The presence of qualifying words indicates that the author is taking special care with their words, which is certainly important when composing the right answer. After all, there are many ways to be wrong, but there is only one way to be right! For this reason, it is wise to avoid answers that are absolute when taking a multiple-choice test. An absolute answer is one that says things are either all one way or all another. They often include words like *every*, *always*, *best*, and *never*. If you are taking a multiple-choice test in a subject that doesn't lend itself to absolute answers, be on your guard if you see any of these words.

12. Long Answers

In many subject areas, the answers are not simple. As already mentioned, the right answer often requires hedges. Another common feature of the answers to a complex or subjective question are qualifying clauses, which are groups of words that subtly modify the meaning of the sentence. If the question or answer choice describes a rule to which there are exceptions or the subject matter is complicated, ambiguous, or confusing, the correct answer will require many words in order to be expressed clearly and accurately. In essence, you should not be deterred by answer choices that seem

5

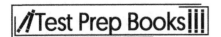
excessively long. Oftentimes, the author of the text will not be able to write the correct answer without offering some qualifications and modifications. Your job is to read the answer choices thoroughly and completely and to select the one that most accurately and precisely answers the question.

13. Restating to Understand

Sometimes, a question on a multiple-choice test is difficult not because of what it asks but because of how it is written. If this is the case, restate the question or answer choice in different words. This process serves a couple of important purposes. First, it forces you to concentrate on the core of the question. In order to rephrase the question accurately, you have to understand it well. Rephrasing the question will concentrate your mind on the key words and ideas. Second, it will present the information to your mind in a fresh way. This process may trigger your memory and render some useful scrap of information picked up while studying.

14. True Statements

Sometimes an answer choice will be true in itself, but it does not answer the question. This is one of the main reasons why it is essential to read the question carefully and completely before proceeding to the answer choices. Too often, test takers skip ahead to the answer choices and look for true statements. Having found one of these, they are content to select it without reference to the question above. Obviously, this provides an easy way for test makers to play tricks. The savvy test taker will always read the entire question before turning to the answer choices. Then, having settled on a correct answer choice, he or she will refer to the original question and ensure that the selected answer is relevant. The mistake of choosing a correct-but-irrelevant answer choice is especially common on questions related to specific pieces of objective knowledge. A prepared test taker will have a wealth of factual knowledge at their disposal and should not be careless in its application.

15. No Patterns

One of the more dangerous ideas that circulates about multiple-choice tests is that the correct answers tend to fall into patterns. These erroneous ideas range from a belief that B and C are the most common right answers, to the idea that an unprepared test-taker should answer "A-B-A-C-A-D-A-B-A." It cannot be emphasized enough that pattern-seeking of this type is exactly the WRONG way to approach a multiple-choice test. To begin with, it is highly unlikely that the test maker will plot the correct answers according to some predetermined pattern. The questions are scrambled and delivered in a random order. Furthermore, even if the test maker was following a pattern in the assignation of correct answers, there is no reason why the test taker would know which pattern he or she was using. Any attempt to discern a pattern in the answer choices is a waste of time and a distraction from the real work of taking the test. A test taker would be much better served by extra preparation before the test than by reliance on a pattern in the answers.

Bonus Content & Audiobook Access

We host multiple bonus items online, including access to the audiobook version of this study guide. Scan the QR code or go to this link to access this content:

testprepbooks.com/bonus/rica

If you have any issues, please email support@testprepbooks.com.

Introduction to the RICA

Function of the Test

The Reading Instruction Competence Assessment (RICA) is required for candidates who have been educated in California and are seeking either multiple subject teaching certification for elementary school or the credentials to teach special education (known as an Education Specialist). Candidates for these qualifications must pass the RICA before they are recommended for preliminary credentials. It is not required to pass the RICA to receive certification to teach just one subject. Examinees can range from those attending university programs to those who already have college degrees. Between the years 2008 and 2013, 80% of test takers reported having a bachelor's degree or higher education.

The RICA measures whether a potential candidate has the understanding and proficiencies necessary to teach reading to students. It is one of six teacher certification exams in California that are part of a program called the California Reading Initiative, intended to increase the reading skills and performance of students within the state. Evaluation Systems is the company commissioned by the California Commission on Teacher Credentialing (CTC) to help create, administer, and grade the RICA exam.

The RICA consists of two assessment options: A Written Exam and a Video Performance Assessment. Of the two, the Written Exam has a slightly higher pass rate. Between 2008 and 2013, 73.9% of examinees passed the Written Exam on the first attempt, with a 91.2% cumulative pass rate, but only 53.3% passed the Video Performance Assessment the first time, and 59.6% collectively. When combined, the two test versions have a 73.9% first-time pass rate and 91.5% cumulative pass rate. The number of candidates taking the RICA during 2012-2013 was 9,764, which is quite a bit less than the high of 26,000 in 2003-04.

Test Administration

The RICA Written Examination is given via a computer-based format by National Evaluation Systems, a division of Pearson Education, Inc. Once a candidate has registered for the RICA, appointments may be scheduled online at any time. Test appointments are accepted year-round on a first-come, first-served basis at Pearson VUE test centers throughout the world.

Individuals who choose to take the Video Performance Assessment version of the RICA need to create and send in a video recording exhibiting their reading instruction methods and techniques. Requirements for the video portion differ from year to year; therefore, video programs need to be created according to the instructions specific to that program year and cannot be carried over to consecutive years. The video portion requires a registration fee plus a submission fee. There are usually three of four Video Performance Assessment submission deadlines per year.

Individuals with physical, learning, or cognitive disabilities who demonstrate a need can request alternate arrangements with Pearson VUE. Test accommodations are personalized and decided on a per-case basis.

Test Format

The Written Portion and the Video Performance Assessment of the RICA exam both measure the same core competencies deemed necessary to successfully teach reading to students. These proficiencies are taken from the following five areas: planning, organizing, and managing reading instruction based on ongoing assessment; word analysis; fluency; vocabulary, academic language, and background knowledge and comprehension.

The RICA Written Examination is structured as 95 multiple-choice questions, four constructed responses in essay format based on a specific reading situation, and one case study question based on the assessment of a student's reading performance (a typed response of about 300–600 words). Total test time is 4 hours, with 15 extra minutes allotted to fill out a nondisclosure agreement and take a tutorial. Time needed for breaks is subtracted from the existing testing time.

The question breakdown is as follows:

Domain	Number of Questions
Word Analysis	27 multiple-choice Constructed response of 150-300 words
Fluency	8 multiple-choice Constructed response of 75-125 words
Vocabulary, Academic Language, and Background Knowledge	19 multiple-choice Constructed response of 75-125 words
Comprehension	16 multiple-choice Constructed response of 150-300 words
Planning, Organizing, and Managing Reading Instruction Based on Ongoing Assessment	25 multiple-choice Case study of 300-600 words (encompassing all domains)

The RICA Video Performance Assessment allows candidates to be assessed on classroom teaching performance rather than taking a written test. Individuals who choose this format must produce and send in three video packages, each containing an instructional context form, a 10-minute video, and a reflection form. The three video packages correlate to the following settings: whole-class, small group, and individual instruction. Requirements are often different from year to year, and therefore must be based on the guidelines in the RICA Video Performance Assessment Procedures Manual for that specific year.

Scoring

The score for the multiple-choice section on the RICA Written Exam is based on the number of questions answered correctly; there is no penalty for guessing. For the constructed-response questions, each answer is scored independently; the total of these two scores is computed as the raw score for that specific question. The raw scores for each answer are then weighted. The total score for the written portion is the sum of the score on the multiple-choice section plus the weighted score from the constructed responses. These two sections are translated into a scaled score. The case study is scored separately and makes up 20% of the total exam points.

Each of the three video portion packets is scored as a single entity. Two different individuals assess each packet. The raw score for each candidate is the total of the six scores obtained from the various scoring experts. The raw score is then translated into a scaled score.

The range of scores for both exams is 100-300. In order to successfully gain RICA certification, a passing score of at least 220 on either test format is required.

Recent/Future Developments

As of August 30, 2016, results for the RICA Written Exam are accessible via a candidate's account for 2 years (in the past, results were only available for 45 days). Test results for the RICA Video Performance Assessment can be accessed online via a PDF file for 45 days after the scores are released. Copies of test results can be requested by submitting a reprint request form once the 2-year timeframe is over (or in the case of the RICA Video Performance Assessment, the 45-day period).

Study Prep Plan for the RICA

1 **Schedule -** Use one of our study schedules below or come up with one of your own.

2 **Relax -** Test anxiety can hurt even the best students. There are many ways to reduce stress. Find the one that works best for you.

3 **Execute -** Once you have a good plan in place, be sure to stick to it.

One Week Study Schedule		
Day 1	Word Analysis
Day 2	Fluency
Day 3	Comprehension
Day 4	Planning, Organizing, and Managing...
Day 5	Practice Test #1
Day 6	Practice Test #2
Day 7	Take Your Exam!

Two Week Study Schedule			
Day 1	Word Analysis	Day 8	Comprehension
Day 2	Terminology and Concepts in Phonics...	Day 9	Student Comprehension of Expository...
Day 3	Developing Phonics Knowledge...	Day 10	Planning, Organizing, and Managing...
Day 4	Syllabic Analysis, Structural Analysis...	Day 11	Reading Assessments and Best Practices
Day 5	Fluency	Day 12	Practice Test #1
Day 6	Vocabulary, Academic Language...	Day 13	Practice Test #2
Day 7	Promoting a Wide Range of Formal...	Day 14	Take Your Exam!

11

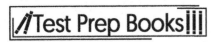

One Month Study Schedule							
Day 1	Word Analysis	Day 11	Research-Based, Systematic, Explicit...	Day 21	Practice Questions
Day 2	Knowledge in Print, Letter Recognition...	Day 12	Practice Questions	Day 22	Planning, Organizing, and Managing Reading...
Day 3	Terminology and Concepts in Phonics...	Day 13	Vocabulary, Academic Language...	Day 23	Effective Instructional Delivery in Reading...
Day 4	Decoding, Encoding, and the Stages of...	Day 14	Student Development of Vocabulary...	Day 24	Reading Assessments and Best Practices
Day 5	Developing Phonics Knowledge...	Day 15	Addressing the Full Range of Learners...	Day 25	Practice Questions & Writing Tips
Day 6	Universal Access and Differentiated...	Day 16	Practice Questions	Day 26	Practice Test #1
Day 7	Syllabic Analysis, Structural Analysis...	Day 17	Comprehension	Day 27	Answer Explanations
Day 8	Continual Assessment for Multisyllabic...	Day 18	Facilitating Reading Comprehension	Day 28	Practice Test #2
Day 9	Practice Questions	Day 19	Narrative/Literary Texts and Literary Response...	Day 29	Answer Explanations
Day 10	Fluency	Day 20	Student Comprehension of Expository/ Informational...	Day 30	Take Your Exam!

Word Analysis

Word analysis includes phonics and decoding. Through word analysis, students figure out unfamiliar words by recognizing the relationship between the spelling and the pronunciation of letters, syllables, morphemes, and words.

Domain 2 of the RICA consists of Competencies 3-7. Collectively, these competencies will investigate the instruction, assessment, and differentiation of the following skills in terms of spelling and reading development: phonological and phonemic awareness and development, print awareness, letter recognition, the alphabetic principle, phonics instruction terminology and concepts, and sight word recognition and automaticity.

Phonological and Phonemic Awareness Skills in Reading Development

Phonological Awareness vs. Phonemic Awareness

Phonological awareness is the recognition that oral language is made of smaller units, such as syllables and words. Phonemic awareness is a type of phonological awareness. Phonemic-aware students recognize specific units of spoken language called phonemes. Phonemes are unique and easily identifiable units of sound. Examples include /t/, /b/, /c/, etc. It is through phonemes that words are distinguished from one another.

Role of Phonological and Phonemic Awareness in Reading Development

Phonological and phonemic awareness do not require written language because phonemic awareness is based entirely upon speech. However, phonological and phonemic awareness are the prerequisites for literacy. Thus, experts recommend that all kindergarten students develop phonemic awareness as part of their reading preparation.

Once students are able to recognize phonemes of spoken language, phonics can be implemented in grades K-2. Phonics is the direct correspondence between and blending of letters and sounds. Unlike phonemic awareness, phonics requires the presence of print. Phonics often begins with the alphabetic principle, which teaches that letters or other characters represent sounds. Students must be able to identify letters, symbols, and individual sounds before they can blend multiple sounds into word parts and whole words. Thus, phoneme awareness and phonics predict outcomes in word consciousness, vocabulary, reading, and spelling development.

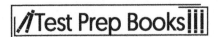

The Continuum of Research-Based, Systematic, Explicit Instruction

Instruction of phonological awareness includes detecting and identifying word boundaries, onsets/rimes, syllables, and rhyming words. Each of these skills is explained below.

- Word boundaries: Students must be able to identify how many letters are in a word and that spaces separate words.

- Syllables: A syllable is a unit of speech that contains a vowel sound. A syllable does not necessarily have to be surrounded by consonants. Therefore, every syllable has a rime. However, not every syllable has an onset.

- Onset: An onset is the beginning sound of any word. For example, /c/ is the onset in the word cat.

- Rime: The **rime** of a word is the sound that follows its onset. The /at/ is the rime in the word cat.

- Syllabification: Syllabification is the dividing of words into their component syllables. Syllabification should begin with single-syllable words and progress toward multi-syllable words.

- Rhyming words: Rhyming words are often almost identical except for their beginning letter(s). Therefore, rhyming is an effective strategy to implement during the analytic phase of phonics development.

Instruction of phonemic awareness includes recognizing, blending, segmenting, deleting, and substituting phonemes. These skills are explained below:

Phoneme Recognition
Phoneme recognition occurs when students recognize that words are made of separate sounds and they are able to distinguish the initial, middle, and final phonemes within words. Initial awareness of phonemes should be done in isolation and not within words. Then phoneme awareness can be achieved through shared readings that are supplemented with identification activities, such as the identification of rhyming words.

Blending
Sound blending is the ability to mix together two or more sounds or phonemes. For example, a consonant blend is a combination of two or more consonants into a single sound such as /cr/ or /sp/. Blending often begins when the teacher models the slow pronunciation of sound parts within a word. Students are to do likewise, with scaffolding provided by the teacher. Eventually, the pronunciation rate is increased, so that the full word is spoken as it would be in normal conversation.

Segmenting
Sound segmentation is the ability to identify the component phonemes in a word. Segmentation begins with simple, single-syllable words. For instance, a teacher might pronounce the word tub and see if students can identify the /t/, /u/, and /b/ sounds. The student must identify all three sounds in order for sound segmentation to be complete.

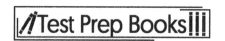

Deleting

Sound deletion is an oral activity in which one of the phonemes of a spoken word is removed. For example, a teacher may say a word aloud and then ask students to say the word without a specific sound (e.g., "What word would be formed if cat is said without the /c/ sound?"). With repetition, deletion activities can improve phoneme recognition.

Substituting

Like deletion, substitution takes place orally and is initiated through modeling. However, instead of deleting a phoneme or syllable, spoken words are manipulated via the substitution of one phoneme for another (e.g., "What word would be formed if we change the /b/ in bun to /r/?").

Differentiating Instruction to Reach a Full Range of Learners

The following strategies can be used to develop phonological and phonemic awareness in students that struggle with reading, disabled learners, special-needs students, English language learners (ELLs), speakers of nonstandard English, and advanced learners:

- Differentiated instruction for struggling readers, disabled students, or students with special needs should include the re-teaching and/or emphasis of key skills, such as blending and segmenting. Such instruction should be supported through the employment of a variety of concrete examples that explain a concept or task. Teaching strategies of such concepts or tasks should utilize visual, kinesthetic, and tactile modalities, and ample practice time should be allotted.

- Instruction of phonological and phonemic awareness can also be differentiated for ELLs and speakers of nonstandard English. Most English phonemes are present in other languages. Therefore, teachers can capitalize on the transfer of relevant knowledge, skills, and phonemes from a student's primary language into the English language. In this way, extra attention and instructional emphasis can be applied toward phonemes and phoneme sequences that are nontransferable between the two languages.

- Advanced learners benefit from phonological and phonemic instruction with greater breadth and depth. Such instruction should occur at a faster pace and expand students' current skills.

Continual Assessment of Phonological and Phonemic Awareness Needs to Occur

Entry-level assessments, progress monitoring, and summative assessments need to be administered in order to determine students' phonological and phonemic awareness. Appropriate formal and informal assessments for such purposes include:

The Yopp-Singer Test of Phonemic Segmentation

This is an oral entry-level or summative assessment of phonemic awareness during which a teacher reads twenty-two words aloud one at a time to a single student. The student is to break each word apart by stating the word's sounds in the order that they are heard, and the teacher records the student's responses. Correctly segmented letter sounds are circled, and incorrect responses are noted. If a student does well, then he or she is likely to do well in other phonemic areas. Upon poor student performance, the sound(s) with which a student struggles should be emphasized and/or retaught shortly after the time of the assessment.

After the Yopp-Singer Test, the blending of words, syllabification, and/or onset-rime identification should be assessed. The last set of phonological and phonemic skills to be assessed is composed of isolation, blending, deletion, and substitution.

Recognizing Rhyme Assessment

Word awareness, specifically awareness of onset-rime, can be assessed as a progress-monitoring activity. During this assessment, the teacher says two words. Students are to point their thumbs up if the words rhyme and down if the words do not rhyme. Immediate feedback and remediation are provided if the majority of the students respond incorrectly to a word pair.

Isolation or Matching Games

Games can be used to identify initial, medial, and final phonemes. During a phoneme-isolation activity, the teacher says one word at a time. The student is to tell the teacher the first, medial, or last sound of the word. During phoneme-matching activities, a teacher reads a group of words. The student is to say which two words from the group begin or end with the same sound. A similar activity can be completed to assess deletion and/or substitution (e.g., "What word would result if we replaced the /c/ of *cat* with an *h*?"). In this way, teachers can assess if **remediation** or extra instruction on initial, medial, or final phonemes is required and develop lessons accordingly.

Phoneme Blending Assessment

In this assessment, a teacher says all the sounds within a word and a student listens to the teacher and is asked for the word that they hear when the sounds are put together quickly. This skill will be needed when students learn letter-sound pairs and decipher unknown words in their reading. Thus, mastery of this assessment can be used as an indicator to the teacher that the students are ready to learn higher-level phonological and/or phonemic tasks.

Please note that student results should be recorded, analyzed, and used to determine if students demonstrate mastery over the assessed skill and/or identify the needs of students. If mastery is not demonstrated, then the assessments should be used to determine exactly which letter-sound combinations or other phonemes need to be remediated. Any of the strategies earlier addressed (rhyming, blending, segmenting, deleting, substituting) can be used for such purposes.

Knowledge in Print, Letter Recognition, and the Alphabetic Principle in Reading Development

Explicit, Research-Based Strategies for Print Awareness

Print awareness, the understanding that printed words carry meaning, aids reading development. Print awareness includes the understanding that:

- Words are made of letters, spaces appear between words, and words make sentences.

- Print is organized in a particular way (e.g., read from left to right and top to bottom, read from front to back, etc.), so books must be tracked and held accordingly.

- Different types of print serve specific purposes (magazines, billboards, essays, fiction, etc.).

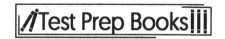
Print awareness provides the foundation on which all other literacy skills are built. It is often the first stage of reading development. Print awareness helps students develop skills such as word reading, reading comprehension, and letter-sound correspondence. For this reason, a child's performance on tasks relevant to their print awareness is indicative of the child's future reading achievement.

The following strategies can be used to increase print awareness in students:

- *An adult reads aloud to students or during shared reading experiences.* In order to maximize print awareness within the student, the reader should point out the form, function, orientation, and sounds of letters and words.

- Utilize shared reading experiences as a tool for building one-to-one correspondence. One-to-one correspondence is the ability to match written letters or words to a spoken word when reading. This can be accomplished by pointing to words as they are read. This helps students make text-to-word connections. Pointing also aids directionality, or the ability to track the words that are being read.

- Use the child's environment. To reinforce print awareness, teachers can make a child aware of print in their environment, such as words on traffic signs. Teachers can reinforce this by labeling objects in the classroom.

- Instruct students about book organization during read-alouds. Students should be taught the proper orientation, tracking, and numbering conventions of books. For example, teachers can differentiate the title from the author's name on the front cover of a book.

- Let students practice. Allowing students to practice book-handling skills with wordless books, predictable text, or patterned text will help to instill print awareness.

Strategies to Develop Letter Recognition

Among the skills that are used to determine reading readiness, letter identification is the strongest predictor. Letter recognition is the identification of each letter in the alphabet. Letter recognition does not include letter-sound correspondences; however, learning about and being able to recognize letters may increase student motivation to learn letter sounds. Also, the names of many letters are similar to their sounds, so letter recognition serves as a gateway for the letter-sound relationships that are needed for reading to occur. Similarly, the ability to differentiate between uppercase and lowercase letters is beneficial in determining where a sentence begins and ends.

To be fluent in letter identification, students should be able to identify letter names in and out of context with automaticity. In order to obtain such familiarity with the identification of letters, students need ample experience, acquaintance, and practice with letters. Explicit instruction in letter recognition, practice printing uppercase and lowercase letters of the alphabet, and consistent exposure to printed letters are essential in the instruction of letter recognition.

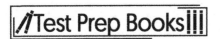
Research has revealed that the following sequencing guidelines are necessary to effectively promote letter naming and identification:

1. The initial stage includes visual discrimination of shapes and curved lines.

2. Once students are able to identify and discriminate shapes with ease, then letter formations can be introduced. During the introduction of letter shapes, two letters that share visual (p and q) or auditory (/a/ and /u/) similarities should never be presented in succinct order.

3. Next, uppercase letters are introduced. Uppercase letters are introduced before lowercase letters because they are easier to discriminate visually than lowercase letters. When letter formations are first presented to a student, their visual system analyzes the vertical, horizontal, and curved orientations of the letters. Therefore, teachers should use think-alouds when instructing how to write the shape of each letter. During think-alouds, teachers verbalize their own thought processes that occur when writing each part of a given letter. Students should be encouraged to do likewise when practicing printing the letters.

4. Once uppercase letters are mastered, lowercase letters can be introduced. High-frequency lowercase letters (a, e, t) are introduced prior to low-frequency lowercase letters (q, x, z).

5. Once the recognition of letters is mastered, students need ample time manipulating and utilizing the letters. This can be done through sorting, matching, comparing, and writing activities.

Using the Alphabetic Principle to Aid Reading Development

The alphabetic principle is the understanding of the names and sounds produced by letters, letter patterns, and symbols printed on a page. Through the alphabetic principle, students learn letter-sound correspondence, phonemic awareness, and the application of simple decoding skills such as the sounding out and blending of letter sounds. Since reading is essentially the blending together of multiple letter sounds, the alphabetic principle is crucial in reading development.

As with the instruction of letter recognition, research has revealed the following sequence to be effective in the teaching of the alphabetic principle:

- Letter-sound relationships need to be taught explicitly and in isolation. The rate at which new letter-sound correspondences can be presented will be unique to the student group. The order in which letters are presented should permit students to read words quickly. Therefore, letter-sound pairs that are used frequently should be presented before letter-sound pairs with lower utility. Similarly, letter-sound pairs that can be pronounced in isolation without distortion (f, m, s, r) should be presented first. Instruction of letters that sound similar should not be presented in proximity.

- Once single-letter and sound combinations are mastered, consonant blends and clusters (br, cr, gr) can be presented.

How Writing Can Promote Letter Recognition and Alphabetic Principle

After the alphabetic principle and letter-sound combinations are mastered, students need daily opportunities to review and practice them. This can be done through the blending, reading, and writing

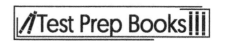
of phonetically spelled words that are familiar in meaning. Daily journals or exit tickets are cognitive writing strategies used to help students practice and reflect on what they have learned. They can also help teachers assess what students have learned.

Developing Print Awareness, Letter Recognition, and the Alphabetic Principle

The following strategies to develop print awareness, letter recognition, and the alphabetic principle within students who struggle with reading, disabled and special-needs students, English Learners, speakers of nonstandard English, and advanced learners have been identified:

Streamlining the skills and concepts presented and reducing the pace of instruction is essential in the development of print awareness, letter recognition, and the alphabetic principle of struggling readers and students with disabilities or special needs. Assessments can be used to determine the letters and sounds with which each student struggles. These letters and sounds should be the focus of instruction. Key skills and concepts need to be supported with a variety of concrete examples and activities that utilize auditory, kinesthetic, and tactile modalities. Extended practice and re-teaching of concepts are beneficial.

When working with ELLs or speakers of nonstandard English, teachers should capitalize on the transfer of relevant print awareness, letter recognition, and alphabetic principle concepts from the students' primary languages to the English language. However, not all languages are alphabetic. Also, key features of alphabets vary, including letters, directionality, and phonetic regularity. Therefore, teachers may need to employ the direct and explicit strategies presented above with ELLs, regardless of age.

Instruction that occurs at a faster pace, with greater breadth and depth, will benefit the development of print awareness, letter recognition, and the alphabetic principle in advanced learners.

Continual Assessment of Print Awareness, Letter Recognition, and the Alphabetic Principle

Entry-level assessments, progress monitoring, and summative assessments need to be administered in order to determine student print awareness, letter recognition, and alphabetic principle knowledge to identify misconceptions that can be remediated in future lessons. Formal and informal assessment methods are as follows:

- Print awareness is easily assessed through observation. Teachers can give students a book and ask them to demonstrate their tracking and orientation knowledge. Similarly, teachers can ask students to identify parts of a book, such as its title or page numbers.

- The Concepts About Print (CAP) test assesses a student's print awareness. The CAP test is administered one-on-one, typically at the beginning and middle of a student's kindergarten year. During the CAP test, the teacher asks a student questions about a book's print. The teacher records the student's responses to the questions asked on a standardized rubric. This helps to identify specific areas of weakness for each student in terms of print awareness. These areas can then be reinforced and retaught in future lessons.

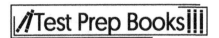

Planned Observations

"The Observation Survey" created by Marie Clay, can be beneficial in the assessment of a student's letter recognition and alphabetic principle knowledge. The Observation Survey includes six literacy tasks:

1. Letter Identification
2. Concepts About Print
3. Writing Vocabulary
4. Hearing and Recording Sounds in Words
5. Text Reading
6. Word Test

During such assessments, a student may be asked to identify a letter's name, its sound, rhyming pairs, isolated initial/final phonemes, blending of compound words/syllables, and word segments, or to add or delete phonemes in words. Similarly, teachers can say a letter and ask students to write that letter on a sheet of paper. The teacher records student responses. In this way, the teacher can identify the skills that have not yet been mastered by a single student, small group, or entire class. The teacher can then use any of the aforementioned strategies to reinforce those skills within individuals, small groups, or whole-class instruction.

Terminology and Concepts in Phonics Instruction

Automaticity for Reading Fluency and Reading Comprehension

Word recognition occurs when students are able to recognize and read a word automatically and correctly. Phonics and sight word instruction help with the promotion of accurate and automatic word identification and recognition. Once students are able to readily identify and recognize words, then they can focus on the meaning of the text and development of reading comprehension skills.

Phonics instruction stresses letter-sound correspondences and the manipulation of phonemes. Through phonics instruction, students discover the different sounds of a spoken language and how a written language's letters and symbols relate to one another. It is through the application of phonics principles that students are able to decode words. When a word is decoded, the letters that make up the printed word are translated into sounds. When students are able to recognize and manipulate letter-sound relationships of single-syllable words, then they are able to apply such relationships to decode more complex words. In this way, phonics aids reading fluency and reading comprehension.

Sight words, sometimes referred to as high-frequency words, are words that are used often but may not follow the regular principles of phonics. Sight words may also be defined as words that students are able to readily recognize and read without having to sound them out. Students are encouraged to memorize words by sight so their reading fluency is not deterred through the frequent decoding of regularly-occurring irregular words. In this way, sight word recognition aids reading fluency and reading comprehension.

Key Characteristics of Phonics Instruction

Phonics incorporates the alphabetic principle and decoding strategies. Phonics knowledge includes recognizing letter-sound correspondence. Students use phonics to sound out letter sequences and blend the sounds of the letter sequences together in order to form words.

Phonics instruction should begin with the decoding of simple syllable patterns, such as *am* and *map*. Upon mastery of simple patterns, more complex patterns can be introduced, such as *tape* or *spot*. The following characteristics are present in an effective phonics program:

- The goal and purpose are clarified at the beginning of each lesson.

- Visual and concrete material, such as letter cards and dry-erase boards, are used.

- Direct instruction of letter sounds is provided through a series of mini lessons.

- Direct instruction in the decoding of letter sounds found in words is provided, such as sounding out letters and blending sounds into words.

- Students partake in guided and independent practice during which immediate feedback is provided. Activities such as word reading and word sorts, which incorporate previously taught spelling patterns, can reinforce explicit phonics instruction.

- Effective phonics programs allow students to apply new phonics skills in a broad range of reading and writing contexts.

Proper Sequencing of Complex Linguistic Units

Research has shown that phonics and sight-word instruction is best accomplished using the following steps:

1. Phonics instruction should begin with consonant sounds. Consonant sounds block the flow of air through the mouth. Consonants can form either continuous or stop sounds. Continuous sounds are those that can be said for a long period of time, such as /mmm/. Stop sounds are said in short bursts, such as /t/.

2. Teach the following common and regular letter combinations:

> a. Consonant digraphs: Consonant digraphs are combinations of two or three consonants that work together to make a single sound. Examples of consonant digraphs are sh, ch, and th.

> b. Consonant blends: Consonant blends are sometimes referred to as consonant clusters. Consonant blends occur when two or three consonant sounds are blended together to make a single consonant sound. Unlike consonant digraphs, each letter in a consonant blend is identifiable. Examples of consonant blends are gl, gr, pl, sm, and sp.

> c. Vowel digraphs: **Vowel digraphs** are sets of two vowels that spell a single sound. A digraph is not a sound. Examples of vowel digraph pairs are ow, ie, ae, ou, ei, ie, and oo.

> d. Diphthongs: Diphthongs are the sounds created by letter/vowel combinations.

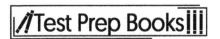
e. R- and l- controlled vowels: These are words in which a vowel sound is controlled by an r, l, or ll following it. Examples include car, girl, old, or call.

3. Teach common **inflected morphological units**, which include word parts such as affixes or root words. Examples of morphological units that could be presented at this time are suffixes such as -ed, -er, -est, -ing, and -s.

4. Present common word patterns of increasing difficulty. Word patterns are made of sequences (or patterns) of vowels (V) and consonants (C). Examples include VC (*ear, egg, eat*, etc.), CVC (*cat, bat, map*, etc.), CCVC (*stop, frog, spot*, etc.), CVVC (*head, lead, dead*, etc.), CVCe (*same, make, pale*, etc.), etc.

5. Teach identification of **vowel-consonant patterns** and **multisyllabic-word syllabication**.

6. Discuss why some words are irregular, meaning that they are not decodable. Students may struggle decoding some words because the sounds of the letters found within the words do not follow predictable phonics patterns.

7. Time should be allotted for the instruction of common irregular sight words that are not readily decodable. However, this is usually not done until students are able to decode words that follow predictable phonic patterns at a rate of one letter-sound per second. Irregular sight words need to be gradually introduced. Words that are visually similar should not be shown in proximity to one another. The irregular words need to be practiced until students can read them with automaticity. New words are not introduced until the previous sets are mastered. The words are continuously reintroduced and reviewed thereafter.

8. When students first begin reading, some words may be decodable by letter-sound correspondences that have not yet been introduced by a student. The instruction of irregular words should be applied to these words as well.

Decoding, Encoding, and the Stages of Spelling Development

Decoding and encoding are **reciprocal phonological skills**, meaning that their steps are opposite of each other.

Decoding is the application of letter-sound correspondences, letter patterns, and other phonics relationships that help students read and correctly pronounce words. Decoding helps students to

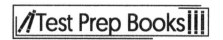
recognize and read words quickly, increasing reading fluency and comprehension. The steps of the decoding process are as follows:

- The student identifies a written letter or letter combination.
- The student makes correlations between the sound of the letter or sounds of the letter combination.
- The student understands how the letters or letter combinations fit together.
- The student verbally blends the letter and letter combinations together to form a word.

Encoding is the spelling of words. In order to properly spell words, students must be familiar with letter/sound correspondences. Students must be able to put together phonemes, digraphs or blends, morphological units, consonant/vowel patterns, etc. The steps of encoding are identified below.

- The student understands that letters and sounds make up words.
- The student segments the sound parts of a word.
- The student identifies the letter or letter combinations that correspond to each sound part.
- The student then writes the letters and letter combinations in order to create the word.

Because the stages of decoding and encoding are reciprocal skills, phonics knowledge supports the development of reading and spelling. Likewise, the development of spelling skills reinforces phonics and decoding. In fact, the foundation of all good spelling programs is alignment with reading instruction and students' reading levels. Phonics instruction begins with simple syllable patterns and then progresses toward more complex patterns, the sounds of morphemes, and strategies for decoding multisyllabic words. Through this process, new vocabulary is developed. Sight word instruction should not begin until students are able to decode target words with automaticity and accuracy. Spelling is the last instructional component to be introduced.

Spelling development occurs in stages. In order, these stages are the pre-phonetic stage, the semiphonetic stage, the phonetic stage, the transitional stage, and the conventional stage. Each stage is explained below. Ways in which phonics and vocabulary development fit into the spelling stages are discussed. Instructional strategies for each phase of spelling are suggested.

Spelling development begins with the **pre-phonetic stage**, which is marked by an incomplete understanding of the alphabetic principle and letter-sound correspondences. During this stage, students participate in pre-communicative writing, which appears to be a jumble of letter-like forms rather than a series of discrete letters. Students' precommunicative writing samples can be used as informal assessments of their understanding of the alphabetic principle and knowledge of letter-sound correspondences.

Pre-phonetic stage of spelling development

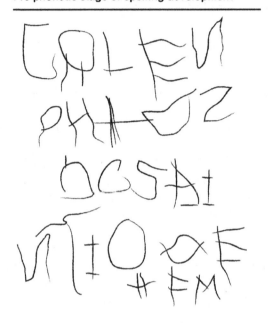

The pre-phonetic stage is followed by the **semiphonetic stage**, in which students understand that letters represent sounds. The alphabetic principle may be understood, but letter recognition may not yet be fully developed. In this stage, single letters may be used to represent entire words (e.g., *U* for *you*). Other times, multiple syllables within words may be omitted. Writing produced by students in this stage is still virtually unreadable. Teachers may ask students to provide drawings to supplement their writing to better determine what a student intended to write.

Semiphonetic stage of writing

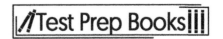
The third stage in spelling development is the phonetic stage. In this stage, students have mastered letter-sound correspondences. Although letters may be written backward or upside down, phonetic spellers are able to write all of the letters in the alphabet. Because phonetic spellers have limited sight vocabulary, they will often spell irregular words incorrectly; however, these incorrectly spelled words may phonetically sound like the spoken word. Additionally, student writing becomes systematic. For example, students are likely to use one letter to represent a digraph or letter blend (e.g., ƒ for /ph/).

Phonetic stage of writing

Spelling instruction of common consonant patterns, short vowel sounds, and common affixes or rimes can begin during the phonetic stage. Thus, spelling instruction during the phonetic stage coincides with the instruction of phonics and phonemic awareness that also occurs during this stage of development.

Word walls are advantageous during the phonetic stage because they provide visual groupings of words that share common consonant-vowel patterns or letter clusters. Students are encouraged to add words to each group. As a result, word walls promote strategic spelling, vocabulary development, common letter combinations, and common morphological units.

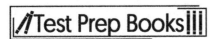
The transitional stage of spelling occurs when a student has developed a small sight vocabulary and a solid understanding of letter-sound correspondences. Thus, spelling dependence on phonology decreases. Instead, dependence on visual representation and word structure increases. As sight word vocabulary increases during the transition stage, the correct spelling of irregular words will also increase. However, students may still struggle to spell words with long vowel sounds.

Transitional stage of spelling

Differentiation of spelling instruction often begins during the transitional stage. Instruction ought to be guided by data collected through informal observations and assessments. Depending on individual needs, lessons may include sight word recognition, morphology, etymology, reading, and writing. Students can begin learning about homophones during the transitional stage. Homophones are words that sound the same but have different spellings and meanings (e.g., *their* and *there*). Additionally, students should be expected to begin writing full sentences at the transitional stage. Writing reinforces phonics, vocabulary, and correct spelling of words.

The **conventional stage** comes last, occurring after a student's sight word vocabulary is well developed and the student is able to read fluently with comprehension. By this stage, students know the basic rules of phonics. They are able to deal with consonants, multiple vowel-consonant blends, homophones,

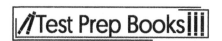

digraphs, and irregular spellings. Due to an increase in sight word recognition at this stage, a conventional speller is able to recognize when a word is spelled incorrectly.

Conventional stage

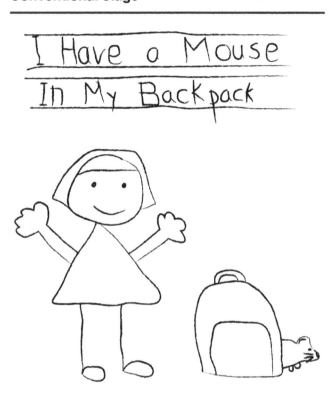

I Have a Mouse
In My Backpack

It is at the conventional spelling stage that spelling instruction can begin to focus on content-specific vocabulary words and words with unusual spellings. In order to further reinforce vocabulary development of such content-specific words and apply phonic skills, students should be encouraged to use the correct spelling of such words within various writing activities.

For even the best conventional spellers, some words will still cause consistent trouble. Students can keep track of words that they consistently spell incorrectly or find confusing in word banks so they can isolate and eventually eliminate their individualized errors. Students can use their word banks as references when they come across a word with which they struggle. Students may also spend time consciously committing the words in their banks to memory through verbal or written practice.

Developing Phonics Knowledge, Phonics Skills, and Sight-Word Recognition

Explicit Phonics and Sight Word Instruction

Beginners: When students begin to read, they progress from sounding each letter's sound out to the realization that units of letters create words. Part-to-whole instruction, during which a student segments and blends each sound in a word, should be applied to VC and CVC words. Next, whole-word reading of words containing single-syllables and some high-frequency irregular sight words can be taught. Decodable text should be used to ensure that students have ample practice with the phonics elements and sight words they have been mastering. The spelling of VC and CVC words is the last area that is taught during this stage.

Research-Based Instruction for More Advanced Decoders

As students become more advanced in their decoding abilities, they will begin to read words that are increasingly more complex linguistically. Teachers should continue using decodable text so that students can continue practicing phonics elements and sight words that have already been taught.

Whole-to-part instruction can be used with students who display more advanced decoding abilities. During whole-to-part instruction, a sentence, a word, and then a sound-symbol relationship is the focus of instruction. Additionally, CVCC, CCVC, and CVVC words that contain common and regular letter combinations can be taught as well as regular CVCe words. Teachers can begin introducing less common phonics elements, such as *kn* or *ph*. It is during this stage that students are taught how to add common inflected endings or suffixes (*-ed, -er, -est, -ing,* etc.) to single-syllable base words.

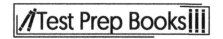

Finally, phonics knowledge is used to spell more complex orthographic patterns in single-syllable words. Orthography is the study of a language's spelling conventions. Orthography includes the rules of spelling, hyphenation, capitalization, pronunciation, emphasis, and word breaks. Orthographic processing requires students to use their visual systems to envision, store, recall, and form words. The prescribed teaching sequence of orthographic patterns is found in the next chart.

Orthographic Pattern	Example of Pattern
Awareness of letter-sound correspondences	Understands that each letter has a certain sound as well as a name
Understanding that letters form words	Recodes certain CVC words like *dog, hug,* and *jar*
Simple consonant blends and matching sound patterns	Recognizes onsets and rimes of single-syllable words like *cat* as *c-at* and *star* as *st-ar*
Recognizing single-syllable words	Uses CVC, CCVC, or CVCC patterns
Ability to read more complex consonant blends	Reads and recognizes single-syllable words like *cross, lamp,* and *track*
Long Versus Short Vowels	Identifying words that contain long and short vowel sounds
Vowel-Vowel and Vowel-Consonant Digraphs	Identifying words like *whey, tree,* and *phone*
Vowel-Vowel Digraphs that have the same sound	Identifying sounds such as /ay/, /ai/, or /a-e/
Vowel-Consonant Digraphs can be associated with different sounds	Identifying words like *cool* versus *boot, harm* versus *hare,* etc.
Complex single-syllable digraphs and trigraphs	Introduction of the *tch* trigraph
Syllabication	Ability to split words into syllables
"Silent Letters" within words	Identifying words that contain silent letters such as *write, knock,* or *plumb*
Blending of two-syllable words	Reading two-syllable words such as *stumble, candle,* etc.
Morphemes within two-syllable words	Identification of correct syllabication of two-syllable words like *post-pone* versus *po-stpone*
Meaning of morphemes	An example would be knowing "macro" means "large" or "great"
Understanding letter clusters	Identifying that the "s" at the end of a word means it's plural, and that the "ed" at the end of a word means it's in past tense.
Syllabication of nonconventional morphemes with multisyllabic words	Syllabication of morphemes that are not pronounced how they are written, like *ance* or *tion.*

Repeated Exposure Through Reading and Writing Activities

The goal of sight word instruction is to help students readily recognize regular and irregular high-frequency words in order to aid reading fluency and comprehension. Several factors affect the sequence of instruction for specific sight words. For example, before a child is exposed to sight words, he or she needs to be able to recognize and say the sound of all uppercase and lowercase letters. Students also

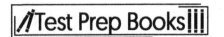

need to be able to decode target words accurately before they recognize sight words. When irregular words are introduced, attention should be drawn to both the phonetically regular and the phonetically irregular portions of the words.

Before sight word instruction can begin, teachers need to identify high-frequency words that do and do not follow normal spelling conventions. Teachers may choose to select words that are used often within their students' reading materials, words that students have an interest in learning, or content-specific words. Alternatively, grade-level standardized sight word lists, such as the Dolch word lists, can be referenced.

Repetition and exposure through guided and independent practice are essential in student retention of sight words. Each lesson should introduce only three to five new sight words and also review words from previous lessons. Visually similar words should not be introduced in proximity to one another.

Sample activities through which sight words can be taught are listed below.

- Students can practice reading decodable texts and word lists.

- Teachers should read texts that contains the sight words that a class is currently learning. As a teacher reads aloud, they should pause, point to, and correctly pronounce the words. Instead of pointing to the words, teachers can underline or highlight the words as they appear.

- Use flashcards to practice sight word recognition.

- Play games such as Bingo, Go Fish, and Memory.

- As students learn new sight words, they can write them in a sight word "dictionary." Students should be asked to write a sentence using each sight word included within the dictionary.

The spelling of high-frequency words should be taught after students have been exposed to the words, can readily recognize the words, and can read the words. The following multisensory strategies can be used to help students master the spelling of high-frequency sight words:

- Spell Reading: Spell reading begins when a student says the high-frequency word. Then, the student spells out the letters in the word. Lastly, the student reads the word again. Spell reading helps commit the word to a student's memory when done in repetition.

- Air Writing: When air writing, a student uses their finger to write the letters of a word in the air.

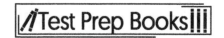

- Arm Tapping: During arm tapping, a student says the word, then spells the word aloud while tapping on their arm as they say each letter, and finishes by saying the word again.

- Table Writing: Students write the word on the table. A substrate, where the word is written in sand or shaving cream, can be added to the table. See examples of substrates below:

- Letter Magnet Spelling: Arranging letter magnets on a metal surface, such as a cookie sheet, is a fun way for students to learn how to spell sight words. Because this strategy is seen as a game to the student, letter magnet spelling increases student motivation to write words.

- Material Writing: Students can use clay, play dough, Wikki sticks, or other materials to form letters that are used to spell the words.

Universal Access and Differentiated Instruction in Single-Syllable Words

Universal access is not a curriculum or a set of materials. Rather, universal access is a concept that ensures instruction is accessible to a wide variety of learners. Through universal access, equal opportunities for all students to learn are provided. Individual needs are identified through formal and informal assessments and/or observations. Instruction is differentiated in order to meet the needs of individuals, small groups, and/or an entire class. The following strategies have been identified to develop phonics skills, sight word knowledge, and spelling of single-syllable words in students that struggle with reading, disabled and special-needs students, English language learners (ELLs), speakers of nonstandard English, and advanced learners.

Instruction of phonics skills and sight words for students with reading difficulties, disabilities, or special needs should be streamlined, systematic, and explicit. Focus should be committed toward essential skills and the highest-frequency sight words. Phonics skills and sight words that are lacking and words that are often misspelled need to be targeted through remediation and routine practice. Concepts and tasks

31

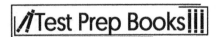

should be supported through the employment of a variety of concrete examples. Visual, auditory, kinesthetic, and tactile techniques, such as the multisensory writing strategies previously discussed, will help to promote spelling and mastery of new sight words.

Instruction of phonics skills, sight word knowledge, and the spelling of single-syllable words can also be differentiated for ELLs and speakers of nonstandard English. For these students, teachers ought to capitalize on the transfer of relevant knowledge, skills, and similar words from a student's primary language into the English language. In this way, extra attention and instructional emphasis can be applied toward the teaching of sounds and meanings of words that are nontransferable between the two languages.

Advanced learners benefit from phonics skills, sight word knowledge, and spelling of single-syllable words of increased complexity. The breadth of current knowledge and skills ought to be extended for advanced learners, and instruction should occur at a faster pace.

Continual Assessment to Identify Weaknesses and Reinforce

Entry-level assessments, progress monitoring, and summative assessments should be administered in order to determine student knowledge of phonic skills, sight words, and spelling of single-syllable words. Below, appropriate formal and informal assessments are presented.

Letter-Sound Assessment

During phoneme and letter-sound correspondence assessments, teachers point to random letters or phonemes. The student is to then say the sound of the letter or phoneme and the teacher records the student's responses. Letter-sound combinations and phonemes with which a student, group, or class needs additional instruction and/or practice can be identified. The teacher can use this information to create lessons that emphasize the identified letter-sound correspondences and/or phonemes.

Phonics Assessments

Examples of ways to test a student's ability to decode words or readily read sight words include **Sylvia Green's Informal Word Analysis Inventory**, **Test of Word Reading Efficacy (TOWRE)**, and the **CORE Phonics Survey**. In these types of assessments, students are given a list of words and/or phonics patterns. Initially, high-frequency words that follow predictable phonics patterns are presented. Examples of predictable phonics patterns may include blending, word patterns, digraphs, etc. The words presented become more challenging as a student masters less difficult words. For example, a child may be assessed on their ability to decode nonsense words. The nonsense word assessments progress from decoding common sounds to less common sounds.

Multisyllabic words within the assessments can reveal how well learners can chunk word parts through syllabication. As with other assessments discussed, the student's responses are recorded on a teacher's record sheet. In this way, the teacher can identify which word analysis principles and sight words a single student, a group of students, or an entire class is having difficulty with. These sight words, word parts, letter combinations, blending patterns, and/or syllabication principles can then be reinforced, retaught, reviewed, and practiced in future lessons. Additionally, the results of the assessment can be used to form instructional groups.

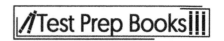

Informal Word Analysis Inventories

These can be used to assess encoding (spelling) of single-syllable words in the traditional manner. Students write the words that are read aloud by their teacher on a sheet of paper. In the early stages of spelling development, students are assessed on lists of words that are common to everyday language, share a word pattern or theme, and/or follow common orthographic patterns. The word lists become more complex as students demonstrate proficiency. The teacher can then plan instruction that targets the letter combinations and spelling patterns with which students are struggling. Such assessments can also be used to form instructional groups of students who share the same approximate developmental stage of spelling to better facilitate differentiated instruction.

As a general rule of thumb, isolated phonics tests should be given every four to six weeks. Spelling assessment can be given weekly or biweekly. Remediation should be implemented when students miss two or more questions on a five-question assessment and three or more questions on a ten-question assessment.

Contextualized Decoding Assessment

Despite the popularity of isolated decoding assessments, decoding should also be assessed in context. The Word Recognition in Context subtest of the Phonological Awareness Literacy Screening (PALS) is an example of an assessment that can be used for this purpose. During such assessments, passages that can be read by a student with 90% to 97% accuracy at acceptable rates are selected. The student reads these passages aloud to the teacher. By analyzing student approaches to figuring out unknown words and student errors when reading a grade-appropriate passage, teachers are better able to determine which of the following three decoding strategies to emphasize during instruction:

- Meaning cues should be emphasized when a student fails to use context, story background, or pictures to assist in the decoding of new words.

- Structural cues are emphasized when a student does not use grammar or syntax to figure out an unknown word.

- Visual cues are emphasized when a student does not use grapheme or phoneme information to decode an unknown word. For example, a student may only read the beginning, middle, or end of words correctly (e.g., read hat as cat). A student may leave off a suffix or use incorrect yet similar letter combinations, indicating that visual cues need to be retaught.

Spelling Assessment

Similarly, spelling should be assessed within the context of a student's writing samples. When a student's spelling is assessed in the context of a writing assignment, a teacher is able to detect patterns of misconceptions and areas that need remediation. Not only can such assessments be used to detect the proper encoding of words, but also student vocabulary, diction, and syntax. By using a rubric, teachers are able to determine the student's developmental stage of spelling. Teachers can then create and implement spelling instruction that targets each student's individual strengths, weaknesses, and developmental stage of spelling.

Please note that once a student's areas of need are determined, any of the previously suggested phonics, sight word, and/or spelling strategies can be used for remediation and/or re-teaching of the identified skills.

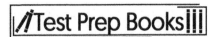

Syllabic Analysis, Structural Analysis, and Orthographic Knowledge in Reading Development

Word Analysis and Word Recognition Automaticity

Phonics and decoding skills aid the analysis of new words. Word analysis is the ability to recognize the relationships between the spelling, syllabication, and pronunciation of new and/or unfamiliar words. Having a clear understanding of word structure, orthography, and the meaning of morphemes also aids in the analysis of new words.

However, not all words follow predictable patterns of phonics, morphology, or orthography. Such irregular words must be committed to memory and are called sight words.

Phonics skills, syllabic skills, structural analysis, word analysis, and memorization of sight words lead to word recognition automaticity. Word recognition is the ability to correctly and automatically recognize words in or out of context. Word recognition is a prerequisite for fluent reading and reading comprehension, which is addressed in Domain 3.

Structural Analysis and Syllabic Analysis in Multisyllabic Words

Reading competence of multisyllabic words is accomplished through phonics skills that are accompanied by a reader's ability to recognize morphological structures within words. Structural analysis is a word recognition skill that focuses on the meaning of word parts, or morphemes, during the introduction of a new word. Therefore, the instruction of structural analysis focuses on the recognition and application of morphemes. Morphemes are word parts such as base words, prefixes, inflections, and suffixes. Students can use structural analysis skills to find familiar word parts within an unfamiliar word in order to decode the word and determine the definition of the new word. Identification and association of such word segments also aids the proper pronunciation and spelling of new multisyllabic words.

Similarly, learning to use phonics skills with more difficult words depends on a reader's ability to notice syllable structures within words that have more than one syllable. Syllabic analysis, or syllabication, is a skill that teaches students how to analyze words and separate them into syllables. Syllables are phonological units that contain a vowel sound. Teaching students how to break apart multisyllabic words into morphological and phonological units can greatly help them not to be intimidated by long words, since these tools will help them use syllable types to make longer words seem like a series of smaller words. The identified syllables can then be blended, pronounced, and/or written together as a single word. This helps students learn to decode and encode the longer words more accurately and efficiently with less anxiety. Thus, syllabic analysis leads to the rapid word recognition that is critical in reading fluency and comprehension.

The following table identifies the six basic syllable patterns that should be explicitly taught during syllabic instruction:

Basic Syllable Patterns		
Name of Syllable Type	**Characteristics of Syllable Type**	**Examples**
Closed	A syllable with a single vowel closed in by a consonant.	lab, bog, an
Open	A syllable that ends with a single vowel. Note that the letter *y* acts as a vowel.	go, me, sly
Vowel-Consonant-Silent *e*	A syllable with a single vowel followed by a consonant then *e*.	like, rake, note, obese
Vowel Teams	A syllable that has two consecutive vowels. Note that the letters *w* and *y* act as vowels.	meat, pertain, bay, toad, window
R-controlled	A syllable with one or two vowels followed by the letter *r*.	car, jar, fir, sir, collar, turmoil
Consonant le (-al, -el) Also called final stable	A syllable that has a consonant followed by the letters *le*, *al*, or *el*.	puddle, stable, uncle, bridal, pedal
Other final stable syllables	A syllable at the end of words can be taught as a recognizable unit such as cious, age, ture, tion, or sion.	pension, elation, puncture, stumpage, fictitious

Teaching Structural Analysis, Syllabic Analysis, and Spelling Multisyllabic Words

The teaching of structural and syllabic analysis begins with direct instruction of morphemes and the six basic syllable patterns. During the initial stage of instruction, the definition and differences of the two terms need to be addressed. The origins of words are also discussed. Students are asked to memorize the meaning of morphemes (e.g., *dis-* = lack of). Memorization of morphemes and their meanings will aid in identification of new vocabulary terms and the spelling of multisyllabic words.

The second stage of structural and syllabic analysis instruction involves the teaching of multisyllabic words that are formed by adding a common prefix or suffix to a base word. Online and offline resources, such as dictionaries and thesauruses, can be used as tools to provide information about the morphemes and syllables within words. Prefixes, suffixes, and bases can be written on sticky notes. The sticky notes can be rearranged in order to form multisyllabic words.

Next, students are asked to identify the morphemes and syllables in words. This can be done via whole-to-part instruction. Students underline words within sentences that share the same prefix, suffix, or root. Then, the students read the underlined words to identify commonalities. Prefixes are usually the first to be spotted by young readers, followed by suffixes. Contextual clues and scaffolding provided by the teacher are used to derive a definition of the underlined or highlighted morpheme(s). Similarly, students can be asked to break all the syllables apart so that the entire words' definitions can be inferred.

Finally, students are taught how to use their obtained knowledge of structural analysis and syllable patterns to spell multisyllabic words.

Relationship Between Orthography and Word Analysis

Orthographic processing has to do with the formation, storage, and retrieval of orthographic representations. Orthographic representations may include letter formation, letter position within a word, and/or letter patterns. Orthographic information that is stored and memorized, such as the correct spelling of a word, is known as orthographic knowledge. Orthographic knowledge, word analysis, and word recognition are interdependent on one another.

Before students are asked to spell multisyllabic words, systematic and explicit instruction of orthographic knowledge and word analysis should be provided. For example, students should be taught how to spell phonograms. Phonograms are combinations of letters that represent a single sound. Examples of phonograms are -*ight, -ough*, and -*tion.* Secondly, students need direct instruction of common orthographic rules, such as changing the -*y* at the end of a word to an -*ies* in order to make the word plural. Thirdly, students should be able to readily identify and differentiate between common homophones. Homophones are pronounced the same way but differ in meaning and/or spelling (e.g., *to, too,* and *two*).

Steps to spelling multisyllabic words may need to be identified, modeled, and practiced with scaffolded support for beginning spellers. The following are examples of steps that teachers may find helpful in the instruction of multisyllabic words:

1. Say the word.
2. Say the word parts that form the word.
3. Spell and write each word part separately.
4. Check the spelling of the word by reading the word aloud.

For some students, word mapping is a helpful strategy for spelling multisyllabic words. During this strategy, students are first asked to say and write the syllables within a multisyllabic word. Lines are drawn for each syllable identified within the word. The word parts are then written on their associated lines. Lastly, the word segments on each line are put together in order to write the complete word. An example of this strategy for the word *bright* is depicted below.

<u>br</u> __ __

<u>br</u> <u>igh</u> __

<u>br</u> <u>igh</u> <u>t</u>

Students need frequent opportunities to practice and extend their syllabic analysis skills, structural analysis skills, and orthographic knowledge in their reading and writing.

New neurological pathways are formed in the brain as new information and skills are learned. These neurological pathways are strengthened through the consistent exposure to and application of new information and/or skills. Therefore, frequent exposure and practice of syllabic analysis skills, structural analysis skills, and orthographic knowledge should be incorporated within lessons.

For example, teachers and/or students should read texts that contain affixes, syllable patters, and/or orthographic patterns that have already been taught or that are currently being taught. Guided information processing, visualization, and manipulation are helpful in the identification of syllables and morphemes. This can be done through text, word diagrams, graphic organizers, word sorting games, or cutting apart word cards into syllables. Thirdly, students should be asked to apply their knowledge of more complex orthographic patterns and spelling of multisyllabic words through frequent and engaging writing activities, such as daily journal responses.

Universal Access and Differentiated Instruction for Multisyllabic Words

Syllabic and structural analysis and orthographic knowledge must support the decoding and spelling of multisyllabic words and words that follow more complex orthographic patterns or rules among a full range of learners in the classroom. In this section, differentiated strategies are identified that promote these skills in students who struggle with reading, disabled and special-needs students, English-language learners (ELLs), speakers of nonstandard English, and advanced learners.

Instruction in these areas for students who struggle with reading, disabled students, or students with special needs should be streamlined, systematic, and explicit. Focus should be committed toward essential skills and knowledge. For example, emphasis should be placed on syllable patterns, affixes, and related orthographic patterns that occur with the highest frequencies. Such instruction should occur frequently and at predictable times. Concepts and skills that are lacking in these students should be targeted through remediation and routine practice that employs a variety of concrete examples. Visual, auditory, kinesthetic, and tactile techniques should be used when providing additional oral practice with new words. Oral practice can occur through purposeful listening, language interactions, and shared reading or writing experiences.

Instruction of these areas can also be differentiated for ELLs and speakers of nonstandard English. For these students, teachers should capitalize on the transfer of related syllabic and structural analysis and/or orthographic knowledge from a student's primary language into the English language. In this way, extra attention and instructional emphasis can be applied toward the direct instruction of nontransferable roots and affixes.

Advanced learners benefit from phonics skills, sight word knowledge, and spelling of single-syllable words with increased complexity. The breadth of current knowledge and skills should be extended, and instruction should occur at a faster pace.

Continual Assessment for Multisyllabic/Complex Words

Effective instruction cannot begin until a teacher is aware of what students already know and what they are ready to learn about syllabic analysis, structural analysis, orthographic knowledge, spelling of multisyllabic words, and spelling of words that follow more complex orthographic patterns or rules. Therefore, entry-level assessments, progress monitoring, and summative assessments of these skills need to occur. In this way, a teacher is able to identify the skills and/or concepts to implement in future lessons. Below, appropriate formal and informal assessments for such purposes are presented.

Please note that student results for any of the below assessments should be recorded, analyzed, and used to determine if students demonstrate mastery over the assessed skill and/or identify the needs of students. If mastery is not demonstrated, then the assessments should be used to determine with which skill(s) each student struggles. The assessments can then be used to plan targeted small-group or individualized instruction, or to form instructional groups with students at approximately the same developmental stage to facilitate differentiated instruction. Any of the strategies earlier addressed can be used for such purposes.

Structural and syllabic analysis can be assessed through teacher-made inventories. For example, students may be asked to divide compound words or multisyllabic words, which can be done by writing each word on a separate index card. Students can then use scissors to cut between the syllables of the words. Alternatively, students may be asked to highlight or circle morphemes within a word.

Formative assessment of syllabication is easily addressed through the clapping, stomping, or snapping of each syllable in a word. During this strategy, a teacher says a word and asks students to do likewise. Upon the choral response, students are to clap as each syllable in the word is said. Teachers can readily identify which students need remediation in the identification of specific syllables and provide immediate feedback. Speed drills and/or advanced word structure analysis are two types of assessments that can be used to assess student knowledge of syllabication and structural analysis. Each strategy is explained below:

- Speed drills: Speed drills are timed readings of syllables or syllable-spelling patterns (e.g., consonant-le) that are read by each student in random order. The test must be administered one-on-one. The drill should be composed of syllables or words that have already been introduced and practiced by a class. During the assessment, each student is given one minute to read as many syllables or words on the drill as possible. The teacher records the syllables or words mispronounced by each student. The teacher can then identify which syllables or syllable-spelling patterns require remediation, instruction, or re-teaching for each student. Additionally, teachers may choose to have students graph the number of syllables or words they read correctly in order to track their progress over time.

- Advanced Word Structure Assessment: In an Advanced Word Structure Assessment, students are given a series of multiple-choice questions. In each question, students are asked to identify which option correctly divides the word into its syllables. This type of assessment can be used as both a pre-test and post-test in order for a teacher to determine which words and syllable patterns should be instructed or remediated.

Phonics and syllable surveys are used to determine which phonics correspondences and syllable-spelling conventions a student can or cannot read so that instruction and/or remediation can concentrate on the correspondences and conventions students have yet to master. In such an inventory, the series of decoding tasks is organized according to basic English syllable-spelling conventions. Such conventions may include vowels in closed syllables, long vowels in VCe, many vowel team syllables, vowel -r syllables, and consonant –le syllables. Closed syllables may be tested out of the context of multisyllabic words, but open syllables are not.

Assessment of orthographic knowledge and/or spelling of multisyllabic words may include observations of students' writing samples and reading, writing and spelling inventories, and portfolios of accumulated words. Unedited drafts and daily journals are excellent writing resources to use for the information

38

observation of orthographic knowledge. A rubric such as that displayed in Competency 6 can be used to evaluate contextual spelling and analyze skills with which students struggle. Observation of students reading words and text orally can be used to assess orthographic knowledge because of the reciprocal relationship that exists between encoding and decoding—that is, if a student can spell a word, then it is likely that they can read the word.

Teachers can use spelling inventories to assess students' strengths or weaknesses in syllabication or structural analysis of multisyllabic words and words that follow more complex orthographic patterns or rules. Spelling inventories consist of lists of words that have been specially chosen to represent spelling features associated with various spelling levels. The level of an inventory selected is based on grade-level benchmarks and students' achievement. These spelling levels are primary, elementary, intermediate, and upper. The leveled lists are not exhaustive, meaning that they do not test all spelling features. Rather, spelling inventories include orthographic features.

Administration of a spelling inventory is the same as that of a traditional spelling test. However, unlike a traditional spelling test, students are not allowed to study the words prior to the administration of a spelling inventory. During the administration of the inventories, a teacher says each word naturally. Syllables are not identified nor drawn out with dramatic pronunciation. Each word is said twice by the teacher—once in isolation and the second time in the context of a sentence. Meanwhile, students are to write the word on a sheet of paper. Results are analyzed using a feature guide. The "power score" of the feature guides is used to identify students' spelling stages and/or orthographic developments. Student weaknesses can then be addressed in proceeding lessons. Groups can also be organized using the Spelling by Stage form and/or a Classroom Composite form.

The results of phonics inventories, spelling inventories, and student writing samples can be used to provide information about students' areas of difficulty. Results can be used to form instructional groups composed of students who are performing at the same approximate developmental stage. Each group can receive a group of words that reflect the particular spelling pattern(s), structural analysis, or syllabic skills with which the group's members struggle.

Sample Weekly Plan

The following weekly plan may be used to target the identified skills of each student or group:

- The students' results are used to identify the phonics, morphological, or rules-based spelling skills that are required by the students.

- Students receive a list of ten to twenty words that reflect the identified skill or pattern at the beginning of the week. Explicit instruction of the identified skills or letter patterns is provided at this time. This explicit instruction ensures students are properly equipped to study and practice the words included on the list independently.

- The following day, students are asked to compare and contrast features within the words. A word sort can be used for this stage of instruction. During a word sort, each word from the list is written on a separate index card. The cards are separated into groups based on similarities.

- Mini-lessons, guided practice, and activities that reinforce the skills explicitly taught are provided throughout the week. For example, students may be asked to find words that match their assigned skill(s) or letter pattern(s) in provided texts. Additionally, games and writing activities can be used to reinforce the skills and/or letter patterns.

- On Friday, a spelling test should be administered. At this time, students are asked to write one or two additional words that were not included on the list. Administration of the additional words helps to determine whether or not the students are able to transfer the skill(s) or letter pattern(s) to a new word.

Practice Questions

1. In the word *shut*, the *sh* is an example of what?
    a. Consonant digraph
    b. Sound segmentation
    c. Vowel digraph
    d. Rime

2. When students identify the phonemes in spoken words, they are practicing which of the following?
    a. Sound blending
    b. Substitution
    c. Rhyming
    d. Segmentation

3. What is the alphabetic principle?
    a. The understanding that letters represent sounds in words
    b. The ability to combine letters to correctly spell words
    c. The proper use of punctuation within writing
    d. The memorization of all the letters in the alphabet

4. Print awareness includes all of the following concepts except what?
    a. The differentiation of uppercase and lowercase letters
    b. The identification of word boundaries
    c. The proper tracking of words
    d. The spelling of sight words

5. When teachers point to words during shared readings, what are they modeling?
    a. Word boundaries
    b. Directionality
    c. One-to-one correspondence
    d. All of the above

Answer Explanations

1. A: The *sh* is an example of a consonant digraph. Consonant digraphs are combinations of two or three consonants that work together to make a single sound. Examples of consonant digraphs are *sh*, *ch*, and *th*. Choice *B*, sound segmentation, is used to identify component phonemes in a word, such as separating the /t/, /u/, and /b/ in tub. Choice *C*, vowel digraph, is a set of two vowels that make up a single sound, such as *ow*, *ae*, or *ie*. Choice *D*, rime, is the sound that follows a word's onset, such as the /at/ in *cat*.

2. D: Sound segmentation is the identification of all the component phonemes in a word. An example would be the student identifying each separate sound, /t/, /u/, and /b/, in the word *tub*. Choice *A*, sound blending, is the blending together of two or more sounds in a word, such as /ch/ or /sh/. Choice *B*, substitution, occurs when a phoneme is substituted within a word for another phoneme, such as substituting the sound /b/ in *bun* to /r/ to create *run*. Choice *C*, rhyming, is an effective tool to utilize during the analytic phase of phonics development because rhyming words are often identical except for their beginning letters.

3. A: The alphabetic principle is the understanding that letters represent sounds in words. It is through the alphabetic principle that students learn the interrelationships between letter-sound (grapheme-phoneme) correspondences, phonemic awareness, and early decoding skills (such as sounding out and blending letter sounds).

4. D: Print awareness includes all of the answer choices except the spelling of sight words. Print awareness includes Choice *A*, the differentiation of uppercase and lowercase letters, so that students can understand which words begin a sentence. Choice *B*, the identification of word boundaries, is also included in print awareness; that is, students should be made aware that words are made up of letters and that spaces appear between words, etc. Choice *C*, the proper tracking of words, is also included in print awareness, which is the realization that print is organized in a particular way, so books must be tracked and held accordingly.

5. D: All of the above. Choice *A*, word boundaries, is included because students should be able to identify which letters make up a word as well as the spaces before and after the letters that make up words. Choice *B*, directionality, is also included; directionality is the ability to track words as they are being read. Choice *C*, one-to-one correspondence, is the ability to match written letters to words to a spoken word when reading.

Fluency

Fluency is the ability to accurately read words at a steady and consistent rate and with appropriate expression. *Automaticity*, a prerequisite for reading fluency, allows readers to apply word analysis skills to unfamiliar words without conscious effort. Strong decoding skills and automaticity enable a reader to focus on the meaning of a reading passage, strengthening fluency and improving reading comprehension.

Role of Fluency in Reading Development

The Role of Fluency in the Stages of Reading Development

The developmental process of reading encompasses several key stages. The initial development of reading skills begins with letter recognition. The second stage of reading involves the decoding of words. Words are eventually connected to form sentences and short stories that contain simple phonics patterns and sight words. Readers are fluent once they learn how to consolidate decoding, sight vocabulary, and meaning context. As fluency naturally advances, readers can dedicate their concentration to the meaning of a text. Thus, fluency greatly strengthens reading comprehension.

Accuracy, Rate, and Prosody

In order to understand the objectives of RICA's Domain 3, the following three key indicators of reading fluency must be understood:

- *Accuracy* refers to the correct reading and pronunciation of words.

- *Reading rate* refers to the speed at which an individual reads within a given amount of time, often measured in words per minute.

- *Prosody* refers to the appropriate use of expression, intonation, emphasis, and tone when reading.

As word recognition increases, readers become less taxed with the interpretation of a text; thus, reading fluency and comprehension improve. When students read too quickly or too slowly for their skill level, they may lose reading comprehension. As accuracy and fluency increase, students begin to read aloud with appropriate prosody, and reading becomes a natural process.

How Fluency, Word Analysis Skills, Vocabulary, Academic Language, Background Knowledge, and Comprehension are Inter-related

Word analysis skills, vocabulary acquisition, academic language development, and background knowledge enable students to read with greater accuracy and comprehension, and at a faster rate. As accuracy and reading rate increase, students begin to connect the text's message to background knowledge. Thus, word analysis skills act as a bridge, connecting comprehension and fluency. The more readers comprehend the meaning of a text, the more apt they are to apply appropriate prosody by using inflection, tone, and expression that complements the text.

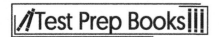

Disruption of Fluency Due to Accuracy, Rate, or Prosody

Poor word recognition, the lack of content vocabulary or background knowledge, and unrecognized words within a text without accompanying word analysis skills disrupt fluency and affect a student's reading comprehension. These factors cause readers to stop in order to decode unfamiliar words, multi-syllabic content words, or complex syntactic structures. If readers stop too frequently, they may not remember or understand much of what they've read.

Proper Text Selection in the Promotion of Reading Fluency

In order to read fluently, readers must be assigned books that match their reading levels. This is especially true of students who are still acquiring basic phonic skills. Students are better able to decode text when reading books that are appropriately matched to their background knowledge. As students begin to implement proper word analysis skills, they'll be able to tackle a broader range of text styles and levels of complexity.

Systematic, Explicit Instruction Promotes Fluency Development

Students tend to mimic learned behaviors. Thus, modeling is a key strategy when providing systematic fluency instruction. Modeling fluency can be done through read-alouds, books on tape, and/or think-alouds. Proper pacing, phrasing, and expression of text can be modeled when teachers read aloud to their students or when books are read aloud to students from a recording. During think-alouds, teachers verbalize their thought processes when orally reading a selection. The teacher's explanations may describe strategies they use as they read to monitor comprehension. In this way, teachers explicitly model the metacognition processes that good readers use to construct meaning from a text.

DRTA, or *directed reading thinking activity*, incorporates both read-alouds and think-alouds. During a DRTA, students predict what they think the text will be about in order to set a purpose for reading, give cognitive focus, and activate prior knowledge. While reading, students then use evidence from the text to verify their predictions.

Developing Student Fluency Through Independent Reading

Silent reading can be effective for developing fluency. However, it's important that students read books that match their reading level. Students who display automaticity in their reading need to be held accountable for reading comprehension during silent reading. Students who don't yet display automaticity may need to read aloud or whisper to themselves during independent reading time.

Promoting Fluency Development

Identifying When and How Fluency Instruction Should Be Introduced

Several factors influence a student's reading development skills. Students learn to read at varying ages. A student's background knowledge, first language acquisition, and family involvement in reading all affect a student's progress. Therefore, when to introduce fluency instruction cannot be determined merely by a student's age or grade level. Fluency instruction begins when a student can use basic decoding skills and can read 90% of connected text with accuracy. Routinely assessing a student's decoding and accuracy skills will help determine when to begin fluency instruction.

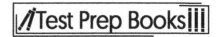

Even if students do not yet display automaticity, modeling can be used as an initial introduction to fluency. Modeling demonstrates social norms of reading rate and prosody while building vocabulary, academic language, and background knowledge.

Practice, Guidance, and Feedback

Accuracy and reading rate are fundamental components of fluency, but it's important to remember that practice is an essential component of effective fluency instruction. When teachers provide daily opportunities for students to learn words and utilize word-analysis skills, accuracy and rate are likely to increase.

Oral reading accompanied by guidance and feedback from teachers, peers, and/or parents has been shown to improve fluency significantly. In order to be beneficial, such feedback needs to provide targeted and differentiated advice on areas where a student needs improvement. It's also recommended that teachers provide feedback that includes a variety of strategies.

Research-Based, Systematic, Explicit Strategies That Improve Fluency and Accuracy

Word-reading accuracy requires that students have a strong understanding of letter-sound correspondence and the ability to blend the sounds together accurately. Providing systematic, explicit instruction in phonemic awareness, phonics, and decoding skills will cultivate such accuracy. When students are readily able to identify high-frequency sight words, their accuracy improves. Therefore, provide ample opportunities to practice these words.

Research-Based, Systematic, Explicit Strategies That Improve Fluency and Reading Rate

Reading aloud has proven effective in strengthening reading fluency. Whisper-reading accompanied by teacher monitoring has also proven effective for students who don't yet display automaticity in their decoding skills. Timed reading of sight phrases or stories also improves fluency with respect to rate. During a timed-reading exercise, the number of words read in a given amount of time is recorded. Routinely administering timed readings and displaying the results in graphs and charts has been shown to increase student motivation.

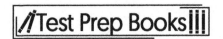

Timed-repeated readings, where a student reads and re-reads familiar texts in a given time, is a commonly used instructional strategy to increase reading speed, accuracy, and comprehension. Students read and re-read the passage until they reach their target rate.

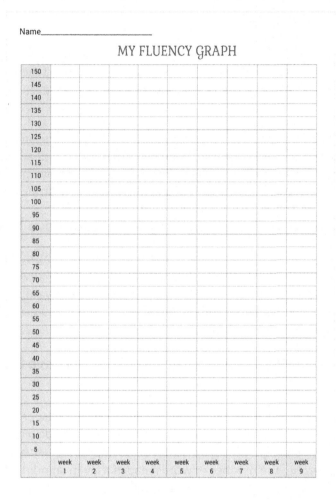

Research-Based, Systematic, Explicit Strategies That Improve Fluency and Prosody

Reading aloud not only improves the rate but also encourages appropriate expression, or prosody. When the teacher, the student, or an entire student body reads aloud, students become more exposed to the use of prosody and therefore strengthen their reading expression. When teachers read aloud, they model prosody, which cues students to the social norms of pace, pauses, inflection, emotion, and tone when reading different types of text. In *choral reading*, all students in the class read a passage aloud together, which allows them to hear text being read accurately and with good pacing and phrasing. By having students listen to recordings of themselves reading, teachers promote independent judgment and goal setting.

Reading theaters also support prosody. During reading theater instruction, students are assigned a character in a play. The emphasis is reading aloud with a purpose. Students use prosody to share their interpretations and understandings of their assigned characters' personalities and roles.

46

Phrase-cued reading is a third strategy that aids the development of prosody. During phrase-cued reading, teachers read a text aloud and mark where they pause or show intonation, emphasis, tone, inflections, and/or expression.

How to Address a Range of Needs

Several strategies can be implemented to assist English language learners, speakers of nonstandard English, advanced learners, and readers who have reading difficulties or disabilities. It's always important however, to provide each student with reading materials and strategies that are appropriate for their specific reading level and area of concern.

Struggling readers, students with reading difficulties or disabilities, and students with special needs benefit from direct instruction and feedback that teaches decoding and analysis of unknown words, automaticity in key sight words, and correct expression and phrasing. These learners also benefit from oral support. This may be provided through scaffolded reading, choral reading, partner reading, books on tape, and computer programs. Teachers should consistently offer opportunities for students to practice repeated reading and should gradually introduce more challenging reading levels as students progress.

English language learners and speakers of nonstandard English benefit from explicit instruction in vocabulary development in order to aid accuracy, rate, and reading comprehension. Providing ample opportunities to read orally with a scaffolding approach also helps this group. For instance, teachers may read a short passage and have students immediately read it back to them. Direct instruction in English intonation patterns, syntax, and punctuation are effective tools in assisting English language learners with the development of prosody.

In order to broaden and enhance fluency for advanced learners, teachers should gradually introduce more advanced texts across several content areas.

Continued Assessment of Student Fluency

Assessment of fluency must include entry-level assessments, progress monitoring, and summative assessments of accuracy, rate, and prosody. The results should be analyzed and interpreted in order to adjust instruction and provide struggling readers with proper interventions. Regular assessments also help teachers to construct differentiated instruction in order to address the fluency needs of advanced learners.

Assessing Students' Word-Reading Accuracy

Running records, widely used fluency assessments, allow teachers to document error patterns in reading accuracy as students read benchmark books. As the student reads aloud, the teacher holds a copy of the same text and records any omissions, mispronunciations, and substitutions. With this information, teachers can determine which fluency strategies a student does or doesn't employ.

Using Timed Contextual Oral Reading to Assess Fluency and Rate

Assessment of reading rate often begins with sight-word reading automaticity. Automaticity assessment may also include the decoding of non-words in order to determine if a student is able to decode words using sound-syllable correspondence.

Among the most commonly used measurements of reading rate is oral contextual timed reading. During a timed reading, the number of errors made within a given amount of time is recorded. This data can be used to identify if a student's rate is improving and if reading rate falls within the recommended fluency rates for the student's grade level. If a student's reading rate is below average, any of the previously identified research-based, systematic, explicit strategies that improve fluency with respect to rate may be applied.

One common timed assessment for reading accuracy is the WCPM, the words-correct-per-minute assessment. The teacher presents an unfamiliar text to a student and asks the student to read aloud for one minute. As the student reads, the teacher records any omissions, mispronunciations, or substitutions. These errors are subtracted by the total number of words in the text to determine a score, which is then compared to oral reading fluency norms. With this assessment, teachers can select the appropriate level of text for each student.

Recommended Reading Fluency Rates		
Grade	Semester	Correct Words Per Minute
First Grade	Winter	38
	Spring	40 – 60
Second Grade	Fall	55
	Winter	73 – 79
	Spring	81 – 93
Third Grade	Fall	79
	Winter	83 – 92
	Spring	100 – 115
Fourth Grade	Fall	91 – 99
	Winter	98 – 113
	Spring	106 – 119
Fifth Grade	Fall	105
	Winter	109 – 118
	Spring	118 – 128

Assessing Prosody Through Observation of Connected-Text Reading

In order to assess prosody, a teacher listens for inflection, expression, and pauses as the student reads a connected text aloud. The Integrate Reading Performance Record Oral Reading Fluency Scale designed by the National Assessment of Educational Progress (NAEP) is also used to assess prosody. Students at levels 3 and 4 are considered fluent in prosody, while students at levels 1 and 2 are considered to be non-fluent.

- Level 4: Reads mainly in large phrase groups. The structure of the story is intact, and the author's syntax is consistent, even if there are some deviations from the text. Most of the story is read with expression.

- Level 3: Reads mainly in three- or four-word phrase groups. Majority of phrasing is appropriate and preserves syntax of the author. Little expression is present with interpreting the text.

- Level 2: Reads two-word phrases with some three- or four-word groupings. Word-by-word reading may occur. Some word groupings may seem awkward, indicating that the student is not paying attention to the larger context.

- Level 1: Reads word-by-word. Some occasional two-or-three-word phrases may be present, but they are not frequent, or they don't preserve meaningful syntax.

Practice Questions

1. What contributes the most to schema development?
   a. Reading comprehension
   b. Structural analysis
   c. Written language
   d. Background knowledge

2. Which isn't an essential component of effective fluency instruction?
   a. Spelling
   b. Feedback
   c. Guidance
   d. Practice

3. The Directed Reading Thinking Activity (DRTA) method helps students to do what?
   a. Build prior knowledge by exploring audiovisual resources before a reading
   b. Predict what will occur in a text and search the text to verify the predictions
   c. Identify, define, and review unfamiliar terms
   d. Understand the format of multiple types and genres of text

4. A teacher assigns a writing prompt in order to assess her students' reading skills. This form of reading assessment is:
   a. The most beneficial way to assess reading comprehension.
   b. Invalid because a student's ability to read and write are unrelated.
   c. Erroneous since the strength of a student's reading and writing vocabulary may differ.
   d. The worst way to assess reading comprehension.

5. When does scaffolded reading occur?
   a. A student hears a recording of herself reading a text in order to set personal reading goals.
   b. A student receives assistance and feedback on strategies to utilize while reading.
   c. A student is given extra time to find the answers to predetermined questions.
   d. A student is pulled out of a class to receive services elsewhere.

Answer Explanations

1. D: A schema is a framework or structure that stores and retrieves multiple, interrelated learning elements as a single packet of knowledge. Children who have greater exposure to life events have greater schemas. Thus, students who bring extensive background knowledge to the classroom are likely to experience easier automation when reading. In this way, background knowledge and reading comprehension are directly related. Likewise, students who have greater background knowledge are able to learn a greater number of new concepts at a faster rate.

2. A: Practice is an essential component of effective fluency instruction. A student's accuracy and rate will likely increase if a teacher provides opportunities to learn words and use word-analysis skills. Oral reading accompanied by guidance and feedback from teachers, peers, or parents has a significant positive impact on fluency. In order to be beneficial, such feedback needs to target specific areas in which students need improvement, as well as strategies that students can use in order to improve in those areas. Such feedback increases students' awareness so that they can independently make needed modifications to improve fluency.

3. B: DRTA, *or directed reading thinking activity*, incorporates both read-alouds and think-alouds. During a DRTA, students make predictions about the text at hand in order to set a purpose for reading, give cognitive focus, and activate prior knowledge. Students use reading comprehension in order to verify their predictions.

4. C: A student's reading ability will most likely differ when assessed via a reading assessment versus a writing sample. There are five types of vocabulary: listening, speaking, written, sight, and meaning. Most often, listening vocabulary contains the greatest number of words. This is usually followed by speaking vocabulary, sight reading vocabulary, meaning vocabulary, and written vocabulary. Formal written language usually utilizes a richer vocabulary than everyday oral language. Thus, students show differing strengths in reading vocabulary and writing vocabulary.

5. B: Scaffolded opportunities occur when a teacher helps students by giving them support, offering immediate feedback, and suggesting strategies. In order to be beneficial, such feedback needs to help students identify areas that need improvement. Much like oral reading feedback, this advice increases students' awareness so they can independently make needed modifications in order to improve fluency. Scaffolding is lessened as the student becomes a more independent reader. Struggling readers, students with reading difficulties or disabilities, and students with special needs especially benefit from direct instruction and feedback that teaches decoding and analysis of unknown words, automaticity in key sight words, and correct expression and phrasing.

Vocabulary, Academic Language, and Background Knowledge

Generally speaking, students who have large vocabularies, diverse academic language, and rich background knowledge are stronger readers. *Vocabulary* is the range of words that an individual knows and uses properly. *Academic language* includes content-specific vocabulary and proper grammar, which are both necessary in order for students to successfully function in academic circles. *Background knowledge* is knowledge that individuals collect through personal experience.

Vocabulary, Academic Language, and Background Knowledge in Reading Development

As a reader's word recognition and fluency improve, reading becomes less taxing and more pleasurable. Likewise, as a reader is exposed to a wide range of texts, vocabulary acquisition and academic language improve. Students connect new vocabulary and academic language within various texts to their own personal background knowledge, and these interrelationships between vocabulary, academic language, and background knowledge improve fluency, reading comprehension, and concept learning.

There are five types of vocabulary:

- *Listening vocabulary* includes words that students understand when other people speak.
- *Speaking vocabulary* refers to words that a student uses in speech. Speaking vocabulary is usually smaller than listening vocabulary.
- *Written vocabulary* refers to words used in writing.
- *Sight vocabulary* refers to the words that a student can readily recognize and correctly pronounce when reading.
- *Meaning vocabulary* includes the words that a student can understand when reading.

Vocabulary Aids the Development of Word Recognition and Fluency

With a growing speaking and listening vocabulary, beginning readers are better able to recognize words they encounter in print. When attempting to decode a word, students work to connect the pronunciation of the sound sequences within the word to familiar words in their speaking or listening vocabulary. As new words become more readily recognizable, a student's reading fluency strengthens.

Thus, vocabulary influences fluency by enhancing automaticity.

Vocabulary Knowledge Plays a Role in Reading Comprehension

Vocabulary knowledge is an indicator and predictor of comprehension. If students find a match between a word within a text and a word that they've learned through listening and speaking, they are likelier to recognize and understand the meaning of the word in the written context. As the students will spend less time decoding and interpreting the word, they are likelier to read fluently and with comprehension. In contrast, if students cannot connect a written word to a word within their speaking or listening vocabulary, their fluency and comprehension may be interrupted. This proves to be true even if the student is able to correctly pronounce the word.

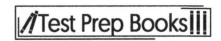

Academic Language Plays a Role in Reading Comprehension and Learning

Spoken vocabulary isn't as vast nor as sophisticated as the vocabulary found in academic texts. Certain conventions of syntax, language structures, and composition are unique to academic language. As students understand more complicated grammatical structures, they are able to comprehend more advanced texts.

Background Knowledge Plays a Role in Reading Comprehension and Learning

Students with background knowledge related to content presented in a class will be more apt to learn and retain information. Background knowledge is developed through an individual's personal experiences. Similar experiences or concepts are retained within *schemas*, a framework or structure that stores and retrieves multiple, interrelated learning elements as a single packet of knowledge. Children who have greater exposure to life events have greater schemas. These students experience easier automation when reading, as they're able to relate new concepts to familiar experiences.

The Development of Vocabulary, Academic Language, and Background Knowledge

As a general rule, vocabulary development should immediately begin in pre-kindergarten and should continue to be emphasized throughout a student's educational career.

The common saying "the rich get richer and the poor get poorer" can also be applied to literacy development. Some students begin school with strong literacy foundations, while others arrive without previous exposure to literacy. Studies have shown that a child's kindergarten vocabulary acquisition acts as a strong indicator of reading comprehension in the middle elementary years, and that by third grade, a child with restrictive vocabulary will likely have declining comprehension scores in future elementary years.

There are a number of effective classroom interventions that can narrow the gap of literacy development, including:

- Regular intellectually challenging classroom conversations
- Varied discussion topics
- Rich and varied curriculum
- Labeling classroom centers and objects
- Fast-mapping (brief, direct explanations of unknown words and student-friendly synonyms)
- Entertaining and engaging word-association and vocabulary-building classroom games
- Daily reading of varied text genres

The understanding of ideas known as *concept learning* and vocabulary knowledge are closely intertwined. As students learn new concepts, they learn vocabulary associated with these concepts. When examples of new words are presented in context, readers develop a greater understanding of both vocabulary and background knowledge. Therefore, it's beneficial to have students exposed to a wide range of text genres at increasingly challenging levels.

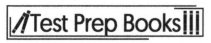
Independent Reading in the Development of Vocabulary, Academic Language, and Background Knowledge

With a positive correlation between exposure to text and academic achievement, students who are beginning to read fluently will likely benefit from ample opportunities for independent reading. It's critical however, that students read texts that match their current reading levels in order for independent reading to have a beneficial effect.

Factors to be Considered When Developing Students' Vocabulary, Academic Language, and Background Knowledge

Words can be divided into three tiers based on frequency of use, complexity, and meaning. A strong foundation in the lowest tier must be achieved before words within higher vocabulary tiers can be mastered. Students with strong vocabulary and literacy skills are able to confidently use and understand words from each tier. The three tiers are briefly explained below:

1. Tier one includes basic vocabulary such as sight words, nouns, verbs, adjectives, and early reading words. Since these words don't typically have multiple meanings, direct instruction of tier one words is rarely required.

2. Tier two is composed of high-frequency words that occur across content areas and/or with multiple meanings. Examples include justify, analyze, and determine. Such vocabulary can be found across all content areas. Thus, mastery of tier two words often coincides with a student's academic progress. For this reason, tier two words warrant direct instruction.

3. Tier three words are words of low frequency and are content-specific. In order to determine which tier three words warrant focus and emphasis, teachers must identify which words are most useful in understanding the concepts they're teaching. Increased exposure through listening comprehension, oral reading, and writing activities will reinforce tier three vocabulary.

Strategies that promote students' recognition, consciousness, general interest, and enthusiasm of words will aid in developing vocabulary, academic language, and content knowledge. These include oral readings of a text, word games, discussions, independent or group readings, and writing activities. Listening comprehension is especially useful in the development of vocabulary, academic language, and concept development for challenged learners and English language learners.

Effective, Explicit Vocabulary Programs Include Several Key Components

Explicit vocabulary instruction begins with direct instruction. Words need to be understood before comprehension or application can occur. Direct instruction is especially vital in helping students learn tier three words that represent complex or abstract concepts that aren't part of their everyday experiences. Direct instruction includes either definitional or contextual approaches.

Using context clues is one well-known strategy for understanding unknown words. This requires that students examine a word in relation to the sentence or paragraph where it's found in order to develop a definition for that word. Students who use context clues can transfer this skill when exploring a variety of texts and genres.

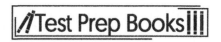

Morphological knowledge development is an alternative word-learning strategy. In vocabulary development, morphology includes the segmenting, identification, analysis, and description of *morphemes*, or grammatical units. Morphemes that promote vocabulary development include affixes (prefixes and suffixes), roots, root words or base words, and the origins of words.

Effective vocabulary programs also promote *word consciousness*. When students display word consciousness, they are aware of the meaning of words and how to appropriately use them. Word consciousness can be acquired through modeling and, more importantly, repeated exposure to vocabulary in a variety of settings.

Student Development of Vocabulary, Academic Language, and Background Knowledge

Vocabulary Instruction

Students may struggle with content-specific vocabulary because they aren't familiar with the ideas behind words. Before beginning a unit or text, teachers should fill in gaps of students' background knowledge and develop definitions for new terms using student-friendly language.

Repeated exposure to a word's meaning within multiple contexts promotes a student's understanding of new concepts. When teachers provide contextualized examples, unfamiliar words are used in a more generalized way, providing students with ample opportunities to explore meaning. Meaningful use of vocabulary includes the implementation of new words within reading, writing, and discussion.

New Academic and Content-Area Vocabulary

Word knowledge, repeated meaningful exposure, and opportunities to use new terms aid in acquisition of academic and content-area vocabulary. Such strategies include:

- Providing guided discussions of academic language and the meaning of new words through the identification of synonyms, antonyms, word origins, and meanings of morphemes
- Creating semantic and/or morphological graphic organizers
- Recording word lists that are presented either on word walls or in word logs
- Finding similarities and differences between words
- Generating metaphors and analogies of words
- Incorporating new words and more precise vocabulary into subject-matter discussions and written assignments

Student Autonomy in Building, Defining, And Pronouncing New Vocabulary Terms

Reference materials are the most obvious way students can independently learn the definitions and pronunciations of new vocabulary terms.

When using contextual strategies, students are introduced to new words indirectly within a sentence or paragraph. Contextual strategies require students to infer the meaning of a word by utilizing semantic and contextual clues.

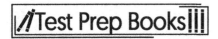
Appositives and parenthetical elements can be very effective contextual strategies. **Appositives** are words that define or add meaning to a term that directly precedes them. An example of a sentence that includes apposition is: "Strawberries, heart-shaped and red berries, are delicious when eaten right off of the vine." In this sentence, the definition of strawberries ("heart shaped and red berries") directly follows the term and is introduced with and closes with a comma. Parenthetical elements are specific types of appositives that add details to a term but not necessarily a definition. For example: "My cat, the sweetest in the whole world, didn't come home last night." In this sentence, the parenthetical element ("the sweetest in the whole world") further describes the cat but does not provide a definition of the word "cat."

Structural analysis skills are beneficial in the pronunciation of new words. When readers use **structural analysis**, they recognize affixes or roots as meaningful parts within a word. When a new word doesn't contain parts that are recognized by a student, the reader can use phonic letter–sound patterns to divide the word into syllables. The word parts can then be combined to yield the proper pronunciation.

Word maps are visual organizers that promote structural analysis skills for vocabulary development. They may require students to provide definitions, synonyms, antonyms, and pictures for given vocabulary terms. Alternatively, morphological maps may be used to relate words that share a common morpheme.

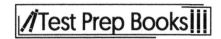

Similarly, word webs are used to compare and classify a list of words. Word webs show relationships between new words and a student's background knowledge. The main concept is in the center of the word web while secondary and tertiary terms stem off from it.

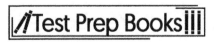
The table below identifies additional ways in which teachers can help students independently define unfamiliar words or words with multiple meanings:

Strategy	Examples
By Definition: Look up the word in a dictionary or Thesaurus. Helps students realize that a single word can have multiple meanings.	Her favorite fruit to eat was a date. He went on a date with his girlfriend.
By Example: Invite students to offer their own examples, or to state their understanding following your own examples.	A myth is a story attempting to explain a natural phenomenon, such as the story of Prometheus to understand fire.
By Synonym: Understand that words have many different meanings. Some words are better synonyms than others.	She was very happy that day; her face was *radiant* with joy.
By Antonym: Teach student to look for words that have opposite meanings if the context of the sentence calls for its opposite.	Hannah was not happy that day; she was in fact very *depressed*.
By Apposition: Apposition is when the definition is given within the sentence.	The mango, a round, yellow, juicy fruit with an enormous seed in the middle, was ripe enough to eat.
By Origin: Identify Greek and Latin roots to figure out meanings of words.	In the word hypertension, the root "hyper" is a Greek word meaning "above" or "over."
By Context: Identifying what a word means by the surrounding text.	Water evaporates when it becomes hot, and the liquid turns into gas.

Developing Word Consciousness and Love of Words

Word consciousness can be developed through structural analysis of word parts and words origins. Identification of word segments will enable students to master new words more readily.

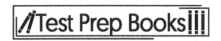

Students can develop a love of words through word games, which create a safe environment to take linguistic risks and feel successful. Examples include sight word games, word memory games, or games that require students to create new words using an assigned list of affixes and roots.

A word sort is an example of a word game that can be used to develop word consciousness. Using a set of word cards prepared by the teacher, students decide how to separate the cards into categories. Students are then asked to explain why they grouped a set of words together.

Students also learn to love words by sharing new and interesting words they encounter through independent reading or by learning new words taught explicitly by the teacher. Students can share new words on an online word blog or word cloud, a word wall within the classroom, or a word list contained within a notebook. These tools help to personalize vocabulary instruction while improving students' flexibility and fluency.

Schema development for easier word acquisition can be developed by dividing these word lists into categories based on similarities or differences. The list of new words should be referred to often in order to increase the students' exposure. To further strengthen comprehension, students should be required to utilize the words in writing and discussion activities.

Listening-Comprehension Activities

Discussing the meaning of literary or informational texts and analyzing word choice will elicit listening comprehension in students. Repeated exposure to metaphors, similes, and descriptive language allows for further discussion of word meaning. When teachers identify the importance of descriptive language within a text, students will often form a metacognitive link between the words used by expert authors and their own interpretation. Such attention will foster purposeful writing and mastery of word choice in students' personal writing.

Providing a Wide Range of Literary and Informational Texts

By reading multiple genres of text, students are exposed to a variety of words and word usage. Students not only begin to internalize how various authors use words, but they also gain vocabulary, learn the rules of academic language, and build concept and background knowledge. This will help students to develop a love of reading and motivate them to independently seek increasingly challenging reading levels.

Promoting a Wide Range of Formal and Informal Texts of Increasingly Challenging Levels

Since there's a positive correlation between a student's exposure to text and their academic success, students should be given ample opportunities for independent reading.

In order to read independently, students must be able to readily recognize frequently used words or quickly and accurately decode new words. Thus, before independent reading, students must be able to confidently execute strategies presented within Competency 9.

Once students become fluent readers, independent reading begins with *scaffolded opportunities*. Scaffolded opportunities occur when a teacher helps students by giving them support, suggesting

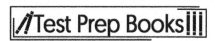

strategies, and offering immediate feedback. Less scaffolding is required as a student becomes a more independent reader.

Students who don't yet display automaticity may need to read aloud or whisper to themselves during independent reading time. Independent silent reading accompanied by comprehension accountability is an appropriate strategy for students who demonstrate automaticity in their decoding skills.

Developing Knowledge of Language that Supports Comprehension

Developing a knowledge of syntax aids the development of student word knowledge and language structures. *Syntactic awareness* is the ability to change the order of words within a sentence without losing the meaning of the original sentence. It contributes to the process of inferring the meaning of new words from the context of a sentence or paragraph. Syntactic awareness has been shown to increase reading comprehension and writing skills. The following strategies can be used to develop syntactic awareness:

- Combining sentences requires students to develop the ability to write compound sentences. This process develops word choice and the use of transition words.

- Re-ordering and reconstructing sentences build understanding of the importance of word order.

- The identification of signal words can cue a text's structure.

Through direct instruction and discussion, students become more conscious of word use and how proper grammar and punctuation are used to fit words together.

Cohesion and coherence in written and oral language is achieved through a full understanding of syntax, semantics, grammar, and punctuation. *Coherence* is the way language is comprehended by a reader based on the semantic configuration of the words and concepts, sentences, paragraphs, and sections of a piece of writing. *Cohesion* is the formal grammatical and lexical relationships between different elements of a text that hold it together. Cohesion includes formal linguistic features such as repetition, reference, conjunction, and substitution.

Differences Between Spoken and Written Language

There are marked differences in the vocabulary used within the syntax of spoken and written language. Written language typically utilizes a richer vocabulary than oral language. Because of contextual factors, precise word choice isn't an essential skill in conversation. For example, one can utilize prosody and body language to complement the meaning of words in a conversation. On the other hand, written language is typically decontextualized. Thus, in order to accurately portray the author's message, written language is more dependent upon the correct application of precise vocabulary.

Although students are usually familiar with the rules of verbal language, precise word choice within written language may need to be addressed. This can be done via oral rehearsal in preparation for writing. Students also benefit from instruction of written language structure and conventions such as the effect of punctuation on a text's meaning.

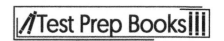

Addressing the Full Range of Learners in the Classroom to Develop Vocabulary, Academic Language, and Background Knowledge

Below are strategies for students who have reading difficulties or disabilities, special needs students, English language learners, speakers of nonstandard English, and advanced learners.

For these students, being selective in assignments, re-teaching, and providing additional practice is imperative. Only select essential vocabulary is needed for concept development. The chosen words and concepts must be supplemented with a variety of concrete examples. Students must be able to use the selected vocabulary terms and concepts using several different modalities. Vocabulary, language structures, and concepts may need to be retaught with scaffolded oral and written practice.

For English language learners and speakers of nonstandard English, it's important to assess their knowledge of basic and functional grammar. In this way, the students' current language skills can be applied and reinforced to facilitate reading comprehension in the new language. Cognates, morphological knowledge, and prior knowledge of grammatical skills in their native tongue can bridge prior knowledge of vocabulary words or concepts in the new language. Once basic vocabulary and grammatical properties are mastered, more complex texts can be emphasized. Pictures, charts, word organizers, graphic organizers, and other visual aids can be used to contextualize these texts.

Instruction in vocabulary, academic language, and background knowledge also must be altered for advanced learners. The pace and complexity of instruction may need to be increased for the advanced learner. Likewise, the breadth and depth of instruction may need to be increased by building on and extending current knowledge within assignments.

Regardless of the type of learner, direct instruction through the gradual release model is a research-based strategy shown to be effective in the instruction of vocabulary, academic language, and background knowledge. This method has four key stages, which are identified in the graphic below:

Continual Assessment of Vocabulary, Academic Language, and Background Knowledge

In order to track the student progress, teachers must administer entry-level assessments, progress monitoring, and summative assessments.

Often vocabulary and academic language are assessed independently using a multiple-choice task, a fill-in-the-blank task, a true or false task, or a matching task. When creating such tests, it's important that the questions reflect the language and instructional format used in the classroom, that the word selection within the tests is relevant to the topic, and that the questions don't reflect exact repetition of something done previously in class. Such teacher-made assessments may be useful as pre-tests in order to give teachers a general understanding of the background knowledge that students bring to a unit. In this way, the teacher can determine the best depth and breadth of concept knowledge to provide in order to aid student understanding of the terms.

These modes of vocabulary assessment are nevertheless shallow measurements of students' word knowledge. An alternative format is a *cloze test*, which requires students to insert words that have been omitted from a 250-word passage at their instructional reading level. Students must use semantics, syntactic, and background information in order to determine which word would best complete the sentence.

Students may know the definition of new words, but not how to utilize them within proper context. Thus, an option for monitoring progress of vocabulary and academic language is to require the students to utilize a set of terms within a written portion of a larger activity.

Throughout a unit, it's beneficial to frequently monitor vocabulary and academic language acquisition. This can be done through discussions or identifying synonyms, antonyms, metaphors, or analogies of

62

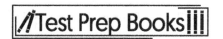

new terms. Students should then be asked to relate the new terms or concepts to ideas that have been previously presented within the course and are then asked to complete a word sort. During a word sort, students are given a stack of cards with a different vocabulary term on each card. The students are to sort the cards into groups and explain why such groups were made based on similarities or differences.

Students' use of words within their portfolios, word games, discussions, assessments, and journals can be tracked using an observation journal that serves as an informal assessment. A separate page within a grade book or a separate rubric can be kept for each student. Alternatively, teachers can create a single checklist that contains all student names to easily access personalized anecdotal records on each student. In this way, differentiated interventions or extensions can easily be made for each student.

WORD	JON	MASON	DANIEL
1. exponent	DWT	DWT	DWT
2. sacrifice	DWT	DWT	DWT
3. tranquility	DWT	DWT	DWT
4. stereotype	DWT	DWT	DWT
5. protagonist	DWT	DWT	
6. introspection	DWT	DWT	DWT
7. hypocrisy		W	W

D = used in discussion
W = used in writing
T = tested

If students have trouble with vocabulary, *informal reading inventories* (IRIs) may be used in order to assess decoding abilities. During an IRI, students silently or orally read a passage and are questioned about their interpretation of the passage. IRIs may also require students to use contextual clues from the passage in order to answer questions about the meaning of a word.

Many standardized tests have sections devoted to specifically chosen vocabulary from high-frequency graded word lists and academic language used within grade-level national standards. Vocabulary and comprehension scores are usually given separately in such tests. However, since a strong vocabulary enables better comprehension, the two scores often correspond. These tests can be used to provide a rough estimate of a student's comprehension, prior knowledge, and ability to make broad associations between known and new words. Examples of standardized tests for vocabulary, academic language, and background knowledge include:

- *The Peabody Picture Vocabulary Test-Revised* (PPVT-R) is a standardized individual test that assesses vocabulary. During a PPVT-R, terms are read aloud by a teacher with proper pronunciation while four black-and-white pictures are shown to the student. The student must choose the picture that best represents the term. As this is an oral assessment, the PPVT-R rules out decoding problems. When supplemented with probes that investigate the reason(s) why a student made a particular selection, PPVT-Rs can reveal a student's prior knowledge.

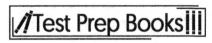

- *The Stanford Diagnostic Reading Tests* may be used to diagnose auditory vocabulary or structural analysis.

  - The Stanford Auditory Vocabulary test assesses student academic language in the core content areas.

  - The Stanford Structural Analysis measures students' abilities to use morphemes, syllables, and other word parts.

- *The Durrell Analysis of Reading Difficulty* (DARD) is used to gauge a student's reading achievements and weaknesses through a series of subtests. During the Listening Vocabulary subtest, the teacher reads one word at a time. The student has to assign each word to the category by pointing to one of three pictures. These words are also used in the DARD's Word Recognition/Word Analysis subtest. In this way, both reading and listening vocabulary can be compared.

Assessment Results can Determine Student Progress and Help Teachers Plan Effective Instruction

There are several ways in which the results of these assessments can be interpreted in order to direct a teacher's decisions.

Students who appear to struggle but they may actually struggle with appropriate pacing during an assessment. If a student correctly responds to 50 out of 100 questions, the teacher should first determine whether or not the student simply needs more time. Providing extended time on an assessment will help the teacher best assess the student's needs.

Students who appear to struggle with vocabulary may actually struggle to correctly decode words. Having students read missed test items aloud will help differentiate the root of their struggles. If teachers suspect a problem decoding words, they may ask a student to choose a correct synonym of that word in order to determine comprehension.

If a student defines a given word but struggles to incorporate it in linguistic production, the student hasn't mastered complete acquisition of the term. In this case, additional instruction, exposure, and practice with the words are needed.

Sometimes students are able to decode a word but cannot match it with its correct meaning, which may be an indication of limited background knowledge. Thus, teachers need to fill in gaps of background knowledge before beginning a new text.

When a student understands the concepts within a text but not the specific vocabulary, direct and specific vocabulary instruction may be beneficial. Should students fail to use contextual clues, which is often the case when students incorrectly answer questions about vocabulary items that are explicitly explained in the text, remediation may be necessary. Some effective forms of remediation include locating and underlining the word, rereading the sentences that surround the word, and re-answering the question. Teachers may also choose to use probing questions if the word or phrase is implicitly defined in the context.

64

Sometimes during an IRI, a student demonstrates comprehension when the passage contains familiar vocabulary and provides explicit definitions of new terms. However, if the passage contains unfamiliar terms and inexplicit definitions, that student may struggle to comprehend the passage. Such students may benefit from previewing new vocabulary terms and their definitions during a pre-reading exercise. Similarly, such students may benefit from systematic (re)instruction of the utilization of contextual clues to infer the meaning of a new term.

Poor performance on a standardized test may indicate a lack of test-taking skills. Therefore, prior to administrating such assessments, teachers need to explain how to use the process of elimination, contextual clues, and keep track of time remaining on an assessment.

Practice Questions

1. A student is having difficulty pronouncing a word that she comes across when reading aloud. Which of the following is most likely NOT a reason for the difficulty that the student is experiencing?
    a. Poor word recognition
    b. A lack of content vocabulary
    c. Inadequate background knowledge
    d. Repeated readings

2. Which is the largest contributor to the development of students' written vocabulary?
    a. Reading
    b. Directed reading
    c. Direct teaching
    d. Modeling

3. The study of roots, suffixes, and prefixes is called what?
    a. Listening comprehension
    b. Word consciousness
    c. Word morphology
    d. Textual analysis

4. A student's understanding of vocabulary found in a science textbook is most dependent upon which of the following?
    a. A knowledge of grammar
    b. Word morphology
    c. Graphics provided within the text
    d. Writing devices such as dialogue, description, and pacing

5. Word walls are used to do what?
    a. Allow students to share words they find interesting
    b. Present words utilized in a current unit of study
    c. Specify words that students are to utilize within writing assignments
    d. All of the above

Answer Explanations

1. D: Sight vocabulary refers to the words a person can correctly recognize and pronounce when reading. Poor word recognition, insufficient background knowledge, or an insufficient amount of content vocabulary can all affect someone's sight vocabulary. Correct pronunciation can influence a person's skill in spelling a specific word, but the opposite is less likely, as most people can still pronounce words well even if they don't spell it correctly.

2. A: There is a positive correlation between a student's exposure to text and the academic achievement of that individual. Therefore, students should be given ample opportunities to independently read as much text as possible in order to gain vocabulary and background knowledge.

3. C: By definition, morphology is the identification and use of morphemes such as root words and affixes. Listening comprehension refers to the processes involved in understanding spoken language. Word consciousness refers to the knowledge required for students to learn and effectively utilize language. Textual analysis is an approach that researchers use to gain information and describe the characteristics of a recorded or visual message.

4. B: Many terms in the sciences contain morphemes. For example, photosynthesis contains the morphemes "photo" and "synthesis." After being directly taught word morphology, students may be able to define an unfamiliar term by piecing together the meaning of the word's individual morphemes.

5. D: A love of words can be instilled when students share new and interesting words that they encounter through independent reading or that are taught by a teacher. These words can be kept in either word lists or word walls. Word lists and walls help to personalize vocabulary instruction while improving students' flexibility and fluency. Additionally, there are thousands of online word blogs and word clouds that encourage students to share the words they love. If a lack of technology is an issue, students can share new words on a word bank displayed on a wall within the classroom or a word list contained within a notebook. The list of new words should be referred to often in order to increase students' exposure to new words. Students should be required to utilize the words within writing activities and discussions.

Comprehension

Literal, Inferential, and Evaluative Comprehension

How Word Analysis, Fluency, Vocabulary, and Academic Language Affect Comprehension

Word analysis is based on decoding words for fluency and then for meaning. Without word analysis, comprehension is extremely difficult to achieve. Vocabulary, word analysis, fluency and prior knowledge all support comprehension. Lack of fluent reading can impede a reader's ability to comprehend a piece of writing. In the primary grades, fluency and word recognition are taught first, followed by comprehension skills. A vast understanding of vocabulary is crucial to full comprehension. A reader who has a large, complex vocabulary will understand a text far more than one who lacks a vast vocabulary. Typically, the more students read over time, the more vocabulary they are able to understand using context clues; in turn, they obtain better comprehension skills and a deeper understanding of the text.

Literal Reading Comprehension

The first level of reading comprehension is literal meaning. The word "literal" refers to an author's exact message or meaning. What is the author directly telling the reader? Literal comprehension is the direct meaning of the text, which may include setting, main idea, sequencing, elements of story, and cause/effect. Once word analysis is mastered, readers can begin to master literal reading comprehension. When a reader can decode, he or she can fluently read a text and understand its meaning. Readers use text evidence (facts, hints, and statistics, provided by the author to help support ideas or theories within texts) to further understand texts. When students identify text evidence, instructors are able to evaluate and assess whether students comprehend the questions being asked and determine the students' ability to locate answers within a story. Citing evidence is extremely helpful during whole group discussions. Students can note the page, exact line, and paragraph where the answer was found. This literal understanding and response to questions helps struggling readers follow along, while aiding them in the learning process.

Inferential Reading Comprehension

The second level of reading comprehension is interpreting and forming the inferential meaning of texts. Inferential reading comprehension refers to "reading between the lines." "Reading between the lines" forces the reader to make generalizations from the text using text evidence. It is necessary for readers to have a complete understanding of the text in order to make inferences. A reader needs to understand the direct message, and then interpret the indirect meaning behind it. The response to questions may not be directly stated in the text; however, the answer must be figuratively inferred by perceiving the implied meaning. Inferencing may involve details from the story, sequencing, themes, drawing conclusions or making generalizations, and cause and effect relationships. As a reader's comprehension skills improve, their ability to form inferences also strengthens. Word analysis and direct literal comprehension must be mastered prior to young readers forming inferences; students may struggle to make inferences without prior mastery of these two skills.

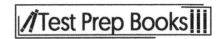

Evaluating Reading Comprehension

The third level of reading comprehension is the ability to evaluate the text. Evaluating reading comprehension builds upon literal and inferential comprehension. Readers must be able to take the entire text and evaluate it for various criteria. A fluent reader may be able to recognize an author's bias once he or she forms and understands inferences. Bias is a personal opinion revealed throughout a text, based on comments or word choices. A reader must be able to evaluate unsupported assumptions, propaganda, and faulty reasoning in the text. Propaganda is meant to help or harm a particular group. An author's personal feeling(s) or bias may be decoded through small details and subtleties throughout the text.

A reader should assess assumptions made by the author and distinguish between fact and opinion. An author's opinions can lead to faulty reasoning. It is the reader's job to distinguish and separate the facts from the author's biases. Readers may also be asked to use evidence from the text to support their reaction to the text or towards characters. Evaluating themes is a difficult task and utilizes a reader's inferential understanding of a text to evaluate the overall purpose of the text. Use of language and the role of text structure and syntax play an important role in a reader's understanding of a text. The complexity of a text may impede a reader's understanding.

Other Factors Involved with the RICA Comprehension
There are other factors that may impede readers' comprehension skills, causing a lack of understanding for the reader. According to RICA comprehension recommendations, students' understanding of texts will be enhanced by instructors who teach syntax, text structure, listening skills, writing skills, and independent reading.

The Role of Syntax

Syntax is the order of words in a sentence; it may facilitate or impede reading comprehension. Syntax becomes more complex as readers grow to learn and understand higher levels of texts. Complex grammatical structures may cause readers to have difficulty with comprehension.

The Role of Text Structures

Like syntax, text structure also involves the complex use and order of words in a sentence. Text and word order enhance a student's ability to read and understand. Text structure can be crucial to a reader's understanding of a text as the English language is dependent on order and structure for text meaning.

Oral Language

Oral or spoken language is also important when understanding a text. If proficient, a reader's speech will aid their ability to understand and comprehend words, sentences, paragraphs, and a variety of complex texts.

Listening Comprehension and Oral Language Activities

Oral language activities, such as purposeful read-alouds, allow students to focus on comprehension skills. Listening skills can promote and serve as a great foundation for comprehension skills.

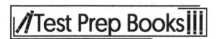

Understanding a text advances students' comprehension skills. When an instructor reads aloud, a student does not need to decode words for fluency. This allows students to listen and focus solely on the text for comprehension. Teacher read-alouds also provide students the opportunity to learn how to emphasize voice and tone while reading.

Text-Based Discussions

Students often participate in appropriate text-based discussions like think-pair-share, discussion time, or buddy buzz. Think-pair-share gives students a chance to discuss the text with their neighbor. Students think or write down their response to a question, pair up with their neighbor, and share answers with one another. Another tactic is to group students to answer questions about a text. Each group then selects one student to share the group's collective answer with the class. Discussions like these give students more of a voice and allow them to consider and unify multiple answers or opinions, as opposed to one person sharing responses with the class. A paper-reading guide also incorporates listening and writing skills. Teachers should provide the guided worksheet prior to reading a text so that students can review the questions. As the teacher reads the text aloud, students can fill in appropriate responses on the guide. They may then use these sheets to facilitate discussions with classmates.

Importance of Writing Activities

Writing is an important component in literacy development. Writing is the next phase in reading comprehension. This level may include summarizing (especially in the younger grade levels), outlining, and responding to questions. Once a student can analyze a text and orally respond, he or she can then write their response on paper. New standards require written responses to texts; the new Common Core standards are putting greater emphasis on written responses. Students are required to answer comprehension questions with a written response style, as opposed to the traditional selected-response style used in the past. Students need to be able to outline and create notes on a text while reading it. In this way, students have the ability to respond to comprehension questions while referencing their outlines. Outlines should include important points, page numbers, and perhaps even paragraph numbers. Students can also use graphic organizers to outline and summarize the text. Writing is shown to enhance comprehension and memory. Simply having students write about what they are reading reinforces text comprehension.

The Role of Independent Reading

Independent reading strategies promote healthy reading for pleasure and enjoyment. Hopefully, these strategies promote a lifelong love of reading. Students should be given 20 minutes of independent reading time in the classroom each day. Teachers phrase this time as **D.E.A.R.**, or "Drop Everything and Read," time. Students can read a book from home, the library, or one selected from the variety of books found within the classroom.

Teachers are required to have a classroom library. Some schools require a certain number of books or filled bookcases within a classroom. The library center should also contain more than just books. The classroom library should be an inviting environment for students. Small lamps make the area warmer—like home rather than school—and provide extra light for reading. Furniture (such as beanbag chairs, pillows, and small chairs) allows students to get comfortable, rather than reading at their desk. Not only is the environment important, but the reading center must also be an organized, designated space. If books are disorganized in the classroom library, students may be deterred from using the space

70

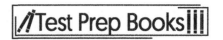

appropriately, simply because they cannot find what they are looking for, or out of sheer frustration. Organizing books by theme or genre helps students search for the books they desire. For students in younger grades, books should be grouped in plastic tubs using picture and word category labels like "animals" or "holidays." This organization method is especially helpful to those learning to read.

A **listening center** is another helpful space in the classroom library. In the listening center, students listen to stories that are played through a sound device (like a CD or MP3 player) and follow along in the text. A teacher can switch the book out weekly to match a theme in the classroom or leave a "free choice bin" for students to choose what they would like to listen to. Again, listening to the story will encourage and emphasize reading strategies, such as voice inflection and pacing.

Having a bookshelf with teacher or student text selections may encourage readers to select a good book quickly. Some students enjoy re-reading a book from a teacher read aloud; therefore, placing it in the "teacher pick" area may encourage developing readers to pick it up. Students also like to follow their classmates. Therefore, teachers should have a section where students can place a book that they want to recommend to their friends. Older students can fill out brief recommendation sheets that briefly list a few of the book's main themes so that potential readers can see if they are interested in reading it. Reading from basal readers and school texts does not necessarily encourage reading for pleasure, as these texts are chosen by the school and instructor. For this reason, silent reading time is so important. Silent reading time gives students options and a chance to make their own choices. Students can choose the book and the appropriate reading pace when reading independently.

Facilitating Reading Comprehension

A reading lesson plan contains several key components. A well-organized reading lesson should contain direct instruction, modeling, and guided and independent practice time. Direct instruction explores the standards and objective to be taught that day. A teacher needs to model examples of the objective or skill and give students a chance to actively participate during a guided practice component. Once the skill has been modeled and the teacher has provided opportunities for students to practice together as a class, students should be given the opportunity to apply the skills independently, so that the teacher can assess skill mastery and students can get a better understanding of how well they grasp the lesson.

Orienting Students to New Texts

It is important that teachers use explicit instructional strategies when presenting a new text to students. Teacher modeling is one effective explicit instructional strategy, wherein teachers show and instruct students how to do something prior to them trying it for themselves. Surprisingly, this key instructional feature is often lost in some classrooms and some teachers do not properly model examples. A well-designed lesson contains several examples. Students often need repetition and to see a skill modeled more than once. They also need to have it presented during the lesson step by step, and not just in a completed form. Once a teacher models an example, he or she should invite students to take part in another modeling example. Then, the teacher may call on students to help show further examples.

Previewing is another example of an explicit instructional strategy. Students can look through the text independently prior to the lesson and develop questions or make predictions about the story's plot, theme, or characters. Textual evidence involves taking phrases directly from the text and using those phrases to predict outcomes. Graphic features can help support students' understanding as well. There are many general graphic organizers that pertain to both fiction and non-fiction texts and some that are made specifically for one or the other. Accessing students' prior knowledge, as well as background knowledge of the information in a text, aids in understanding the text and formulating and comprehending questions. Understanding the purpose for the text and critiquing the type of genre allows the reader to understand if the text is for pleasure, information, or entertainment. Allowing students to preview the text and develop their own questions in a reading journal gives them a chance to answer the questions they feel are important and develop an interest in the text. Teacher-generated comprehension or text evidence questions can be provided to students to preview before reading, as well as to answer while reading.

Skills that Support Comprehension

Students should be allowed to monitor and assess themselves as they read. Graphic organizers and reading journals are great tools for self-monitoring. Many graphic organizers are preexisting and available for reproduction. Graphic organizers can also be student-generated, after students have had enough practice using them. Word webs can branch out details from one main idea. Sequencing graphic organizers can link the progression of main ideas from the story in chronological order. There are also cause and effect graphic organizers to recognize where in the story these elements occur. Fact and opinion graphic organizers can help students separate an author's bias from the facts in a text. Teachers can also create their own graphic organizers and display them as classroom posters or models for students to use as they create their own. Students should be encouraged to keep reading journals and document the objectives for each daily lesson, notes regarding the text, questions addressed by the student or teacher, predictions, and summaries of lessons or texts themselves. Teachers may direct the journaling by providing an objective for the journal for a given day, or teachers may give students several options to choose from.

Supporting Student Comprehension After Reading

Teachers need students to demonstrate their understanding of a given text in order to assess comprehension. Students can meet in pairs or small groups to summarize and discuss the story orally or through writing. Making personal connections to the text allows students to relate to the text. They can also make real world connections, allowing them to personalize the text, which lends itself to better

72

understanding. Venn diagrams allow students to compare and contrast various parts of the text or compare the text to their lives or to the real world at large.

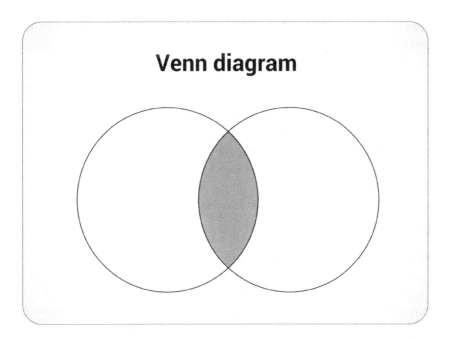

Comprehension Strategies from Oral Language to Written Language

A teacher "think-aloud" is a great strategy to promote the development of comprehension skills and eventually transfer these skills to written language. Students who are allowed to stop periodically throughout the text to verbalize what they have read score significantly higher on standardized testing. Teacher read-alouds help promote listening comprehension skills because students can listen without having to decode the text. Students can freely take notes and outline what they hear, and can listen for reading strategies, such as word and voice emphasis. In small intervention groups, a teacher can read aloud shorter texts to help teach reading comprehension. Rather than having students read aloud during smaller group work, teachers can help promote comprehension by simply having students listen to books catered to their reading level, and then having think-alouds in small groups. Students can complete graphic organizers or comprehension worksheets during listening comprehension time.

Addressing the Full Range of Learners in the Classroom

Students with Reading Difficulties

Meeting in small groups during a reading instruction block allows teachers to focus on particular skills with students that need reinforcement, which helps to meet the individual needs of each student. Rather than teaching the whole group, teachers can give assessments to help break the class into smaller intervention groups based on skill mastery and educational needs. Students requiring remediation may receive help in an individual, one-on-one setting.

Students with Special Needs

It is easier for a teacher to differentiate instruction in small groups of varying levels according to each student's needs. Separate comprehension worksheets and questions can be given to different groups,

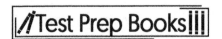

based on ability level. Vocabulary and word analysis assignments can be tailored to the level of skill mastery of the small group. A small group setting is more appropriate when re-teaching or reinforcing concepts as well, particularly for difficult concepts or when only part of the class needs additional focus on the given concept. Small groups can also be used to read shorter books that may help teach or reinforce the given concept.

Addressing the Needs of English Learners and Speakers of Nonstandard English

Small group instruction is beneficial for English Language Learners (ELL), who often have very different needs than native English-speaking peers. Typically, comprehension can be very difficult. Word analysis, as well as identification of letters and words, may interfere with the ability to fully comprehend a text. For these students, fluency needs to be strong before comprehension can be obtained. Although decoding skills take a lot of effort, they should be mastered first for English Language Learners. Even within a group of English Language Learners in a given class, teachers will encounter varying needs and ability levels amongst the students. One student may be working on decoding words while another student is ready for comprehension practice.

Addressing the Needs of Advanced Learners

Small groups of advanced learners may move at a quicker pace using more complex texts or leveled books that are of higher difficulty. Longer comprehension assessments and/or more complex questions with more challenging thinking skills are appropriate for an advanced group. Sometimes, complex leveled texts are included with a school's reading program, located in a school library, or in the Reading Specialist's classroom (if the school has this position.)

Knowledge in Assessment with Respect to Reading Comprehension

Formal and Informal Assessments

Formal assessments, such as selected-response questions, are a useful and quick way to grade students as opposed to free response assessments. However, informal assessments are an even quicker and more frequently used method of assessing students. Informal assessments can be conducted after a modeled lesson and before independent practice. The use of individual whiteboards and a few quick selected response questions prepared before the lesson is a helpful tactic for teachers to quickly survey which students grasped the concepts and which students need additional reinforcement. Those who still need to master the skill can then be efficiently identified and grouped together for a small reteach.

Demonstrating Ability to Interpret Results

When using the results from formal assessments addressing multiple skills, it is important to group students according to ability for the particular skill of interest from the assessment and not just on the overall score. However, the overall score may be beneficial for grouping with regards to pacing and complexity of questions.

Results of Assessments

Lessons and groups should be adjusted to the needs of the students; therefore, student groupings may need to change on a daily or weekly basis. Each student's needs change from concept to concept. Assessments must be ongoing and frequent. Results from these ongoing assessments should be the driving force behind the grouping of students.

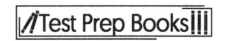

Narrative/Literary Texts and Literary Response Skills

Major Literary Genres

A variety of texts must be used to teach literature and reading. Folklore and poetry both have aspects to enhance comprehension. Poetry teaches lyrical reading and emphasis; it is written with specific structure and rhythm. There are many types of poetry, such as ballads, lyrics, couplets, epics, and sonnets. Poetry teaches students about adhering to punctuation while reading and allows students to read with pauses. A great teaching strategy to employ with poetry lessons is the use of blank poetry books that students can use to take notes and create their own specific poems. Poetry contains similes, personification, and onomatopoeia; therefore, poems are a great way to teach imagery and figurative language.

Drama, or plays, can emphasize voice, and gives students the option to take on a role of a character. One way to teach drama is to divide students into groups and host a reader's theater. Students and teachers have a lot of fun preparing to present a play in front of the class. Prose text covers a wide range of literature from novels, to folklore, to biographies. Developing a unit dedicated to the various types of folklore (short stories, tall tales, myth, legend, and fantasy) can be creative and fun for students. Autobiographies, biographies, and historical fiction can help teach facts. Providing students with the opportunity to research a person in history and present the findings to the class develops comprehension, presentation, speaking, writing, and research skills.

Story Grammar and Other Key Elements of Narrative/Literary Texts

Some important story elements in teaching reading comprehension include character, plot, problem/solution, and setting. Some inferential aspects of reading comprehension are mood, tone, theme, point of view, and voice. These elements are more difficult to teach and for students to master. Repetition and understanding improves mastery of these inferential aspects, particularly when they are broken into independent lessons.

Narrative Analysis and Literary Criticism

Structural Elements of a Plot
There are five main structural elements of a plot:

1. Exposition: This is where the author introduces characters and establishes the setting.
2. Rising Action: This is where the conflict starts to develop, and complications may form.
3. Climax: This is when the conflict is at its highest moment.
4. Falling Action: This is where characters make choices that will determine the end result.
5. Resolution: This is how the story ends.

Characters
When readers compare and contrast characters, it is important that they ask themselves three questions:

1. Why compare/contrast characters?
2. What is compared/contrast between characters?
3. How are they the same/different?

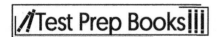

Setting

Evaluating the relevance of the setting impacts a text's direction. For example, how is the storyline affected by the time and location of the story's events?

Recurring Themes

Texts may carry recurring themes like acceptance, courage, loyalty, man versus nature, family, and life. There are many themes that may overlap in a variety of texts. It is important for teachers to remember to coordinate texts with recurring themes in order for students to clearly understand the intent or message.

Style and Figurative Language

Inferential reading and comprehension skills, such as figurative language, involve some abstract understanding of the text. Students must first gain comprehension of the text, and then use their inference skills to further break down the text. Students must understand characters' feelings as well as the reason for the setting. Again, theme is a difficult skill to teach. When introducing a new text, teachers should provide students with a list of common themes to pick from. Figurative language and literary devices can help identify the theme. Figurative language includes metaphors, similes, personification, and hyperbole. Literary devices include imagery, symbolism, irony, and foreshadowing. These two tools help readers interpret the author's theme or purpose in texts.

Oral Language Activities

When students are paired together or placed in small groups, they can share and discuss elements of texts. Literature circles are like book clubs. These circles allow students to speak freely, create their own discussions, and form questions about the text. Teachers can provide literature circle booklets, which may contain response or discussion questions to enhance conversation within the group.

Writing Activities

Writing activities that coordinate with daily skills addressed in the classroom enhance reading comprehension, help demonstrate students' understanding, and also serve as great notes for future use and for class discussions. Composition notebooks can be used as literary response journals. Teachers can also create booklets with questions that are pre-printed inside. These journals provide students with the opportunity to record their thoughts, ideas, or reflections about texts. Teachers may respond to students' journal entries or simply use them as a guide for future discussions. Otherwise, teachers can post discussion questions or the daily journal topic on a projector or board. Daily activity ideas include summaries of the day's reading, discussion questions, comprehension questions, and character analyses.

Full Range of Learners in the Classroom

Students with Reading Difficulties

Small group intervention is necessary for students who are struggling with reading comprehension. Struggling students need to meet with the teacher more frequently and for longer periods of time to remediate skills that have yet to be mastered. Teacher "read alouds" provide students time to listen to the storyline, characters, setting, plots, sequence of events, and conclusions, without having to decode the words themselves, which aids comprehension. Teachers should also play games or complete review worksheets with students in a one-to-one setting because it provides additional time to secure skills and gives students privacy to ask questions regarding the lesson.

Students with Special Needs

Students with special needs may need individual differentiated instruction settings to cater to specific needs. Effective teachers create and use assignments based on their students' needs. First, teachers must identify the skill(s) that need extra assistance. Then, instructors should use short texts at each student's level that can be read aloud and discussed. For special needs students, key elements of a story should be broken down into categories such as characters, setting, plot, conflict, and resolution. With teacher support, students can use story maps to fill in information on their own. As students fill in important details, the teacher can stop to address each before continuing to read, which will allow students to recreate images as the teacher reads. Students at lower levels should support their answers through group discussions; that way, their frustration levels will not peak.

English Learners and Speakers of Nonstandard English

English Language Learners should identify words and vocabulary before they can comprehend. Pre-teaching vocabulary prior to reading a given text can help students understand the overall text better. Figurative language and inferential skills are especially difficult, as they can be culturally dependent. Teaching the underlying meanings of the text is often the most challenging task, as clarifying cultural content is necessary.

Needs of Advanced Learners

Advanced learners should be challenged. One way to challenge advanced learners is to provide texts that may include challenging vocabulary or obscure ideas that require students to rely on inference and prediction skills in order to read between the lines. Another way for teachers to challenge advanced leaners is to expand assignments by adding more questions, skills, and strategies that require a higher level of thought. Activities that promote inferential and figurative analysis skills can create great discussion between peers and encourage higher level thinking skills.

Development of Literary Response Skills

Formal and Informal Assessments

Summative assessments are a formal way of assessing students' knowledge at the end of a unit of study. These types of assessments consist of formal tests and projects that "summarize" what students have learned during a course of study or at the conclusion of an instructional period in reading, such as at the end of a novel of focus. These assessments evaluate what a student has learned, and if he or she met the expectations of what was taught. They are often graded and used as scores in a teacher's grade book.

Informal assessments, or formative assessments, collect information that instructors can use to quickly evaluate students' progress and learning. As mentioned, informal assessments can be used after modeling or direct instruction to break students into intervention groups. Informal assessments can also be used as a pre-screening, prior to skill instruction, to see what students already know about the topic.

Interpreting Results from These Assessments:

Teachers can use formal tests as a way to form intervention groups before a new unit of study is introduced, or prior to another summative assessment, like standardized tests. Formal assessments

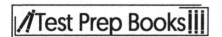

allow teachers to identify which students require further instruction or re-teaching skills, especially before another formal assessment. The overall goal is for students to gain a full understanding of skills and to ensure skill mastery before the end of the grade level. Therefore, skills may need to be remediated and then reassessed. If skills are retaught and not reassessed, an instructor has no idea how a student has progressed.

Planning Effective Instruction and Interventions

Assessments (either summative or formative) are important to develop future lessons in the classroom. Teachers should constantly assess their students for understanding. A teacher should not move onto another topic without knowing if students understood the previous skill. Reading comprehension builds from prior experiences. Texts get more difficult and complex as the years go on. For example, if a struggling student is passed on to the next grade level without any prior interventions in place, he or she may not have mastered certain skills. For this reason, ongoing assessments are important.

Student Comprehension of Expository/Informational Texts and Their Development of Study Skills and Research Skills

Expository/Informational Materials

It is important for students to be exposed to a variety of texts, reading materials, and resources. To become well-rounded readers, teachers should provide students with expository texts in addition to the classroom textbooks. Key characteristics of informational and expository texts include informative facts about a specific topic. Since these are nonfiction texts, diagrams or other graphic aids may be used to assist in understanding the text. Other forms of informational text include news articles, research journals, educational magazines with informational text, and websites. These texts can be used in small groups or can be introduced in whole group instruction, and then further explored in small intervention groups.

Expository/Informational Texts

Fact-based understanding and the use of textual evidence is imperative in expository and informational texts. Students should be able to compare and contrast two different texts and identify problems and solutions as well as cause and effect. Graphic organizers arranged chronologically can help students take notes when covering nonfiction texts. Students need to have the correct order of events in a nonfiction piece in order to identify the cause of an event, as well as the effect it had on problems and solutions. At times, students may need to compare and contrast two texts to identify the similarity of facts, the differences in reported facts, or note any bias from the author. Using knowledge of writing standards and instruction can aid students' understanding of informational text. When comprehending an informative text's objective, students should utilize their prior knowledge of the topic, prior writing assignments, and concluding sentences in the text. This is another example of how reading comprehension and writing go hand-in-hand in the learning process, and how writing and language become important to student comprehension.

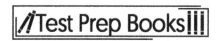

Comprehension of Expository/Informational Texts

Organizational/Explanatory Features

Using and understanding references is imperative in developing reading comprehension skills. Pre-teaching a lesson on understanding references can be helpful, or a teacher may even incorporate this skill into teaching some broader comprehension skills. Prior to teaching from the basal reader, or prior to each story in the basal reader, a teacher should address the table of contents at the beginning of the textbook. This teaches students to use the table of contents frequently and allows them to find parts of a story that they will be reading on their own. When teaching from nonfiction texts, such as social studies or science, instruction should be provided on using the index to identify and locate specific information to answer comprehension questions. Both nonfiction and fiction texts can be used to teach how to use the glossary to locate boldfaced and important vocabulary. It is often most beneficial to identify and teach new vocabulary prior to reading a piece, so that students gain a deeper understanding of the text as they read it for the first time.

Typographic Features

Understanding changes in the appearance of text will help students easily identify important information. Pointing out boldfaced words during reading instruction tells students these may be important words in the understanding of the text, and that new vocabulary may be present. Boldfacing or italics may help students identify when a thought or topic is changing or being brought to attention. Color-coding may be used when comparing or contrasting different parts of the text. During reading comprehension instruction time, it is important to point out when these changes occur. It is also helpful to try to find text of this nature to use in small group or whole group instruction. Text with these types of typographic features assist students on their path to reading comprehension.

Graphic Features

Graphics always help interpret a story or text. Younger learners rely on pictures to help tell the story, while older students use diagrams, maps, and charts to aid in understanding texts. Even for adults, graphic features assist with visualizing the text. Charts and diagrams help organize information into clear and concise patterns. Maps help understand specific places and locations. Illustrations help visualize a fictional story. Furthermore, illustrations with captions help visualize nonfiction and fiction texts, particularly when paired with captions that provide an explanation of why the illustration is important.

Instructional Strategies for Expository/Informational Texts

Structural Patterns of a Text

Teaching students text structure helps them to search for information when answering questions about the text. This again integrates reading and writing strategies when learning about comprehension. Text needs should be written in a logical way. Consistent and logical written thoughts aid in comprehension and help readers find information easier within the text, especially when trying to locate answers to comprehension questions. Students should recall that the broader meaning of text is located at the beginning of a story, and more specific details are provided throughout the text. Subtitles will help students locate information they are seeking.

Author's Point of View

It is important for readers to understand an author's purpose for writing a text. They need to identify the author's opinion in order to appropriately identify the facts that are being presented. Many

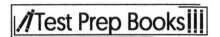

standardized tests require students to identify an author's point of view and perspective and requires the use of inferential reading comprehension skills.

Generalizing the Knowledge Learned from Texts to Other Areas of Learning

Reading comprehension strategies are essential when studying other subject areas. Reading, writing, and language are built upon each other. In addition to these, social studies and the sciences are more complex disciplines that require basic knowledge of comprehension. Students who have mastered areas of reading, writing, and language will often perform better in other more difficult subject areas than those who have yet to obtain comprehension skills.

Identifying Similarities and Differences Between Texts

Oftentimes students need to compare and contrast different texts. As noted previously, Venn diagrams are a great way to compare and contrast texts. Venn diagrams allow students to relate information across a wide range of texts. This helps reading comprehension, as students need to utilize higher thinking skills and identify the relationships amongst more than one text.

Oral Language Activities that Reinforce Comprehension of Expository/Informational Texts

Oral language and presentation are also important in learning reading comprehension. Reviewing and identifying new and key vocabulary prior to reading the text help students understand the text more efficiently. Once students are familiar with new vocabulary words, they should be able to interpret the word in context of the reading, rather than reaching the word and skipping over the sentence or needing to stop and look up the word before continuing to read. This interrupts fluency as well as the understanding of the text. Previewing text and skimming pictures for younger students, or reviewing bold subtitles for older students, can benefit students' comprehension by getting an idea of what the text may be about before reading. There are different ways to find a text's purpose using auditory and speech skills, some of which include summarizing with a peer or paraphrasing the text.

Writing Activities that Reinforce Comprehension of Expository/Informational Texts

Use of writing activities to promote text understanding is helpful for comprehension of expository and informational texts. Along with reading journals and graphic organizers, taking organized notes can help students build comprehension skills. Students who write what they learn actually achieve higher test scores than those who do not. Therefore, students should summarize what they have read in notes or outlines. Note taking will help students respond to questions; it will be easier to locate important information from their own notes and outlines rather than a whole text. The written text also promotes memory of the information.

Additionally, compare and contrast writing activities can help students engage with various texts at a deeper level by asking why questions as well as what questions. Exercises might include discussions of different versions of a story or various treatments of a theme across a selection of texts and genres, with an emphasis on asking why the differences are important and what the authors intend to show to their readers.

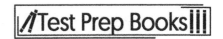

Development of Study Skills

Study skills, such as note taking and outlining, can be helpful because they provide students with notes to reread prior to taking a test, or they can be used for reading or literature groups. Some teachers also allow these written activities to be used during a test for reference. This teaches students how good note taking can be beneficial. Open notebook tests teach students how to take better notes in the future, as they will immediately understand if their notes are lacking information, especially if they are not able to answer the test questions. This allows students to self-assess their note taking skills, as well as enhance their learning and understanding of what they need to change for future note taking.

Development of Research Skills

Classrooms are utilizing more demanding research skills and projects. Science experiments and invention fairs encourage students to develop their own questions and topics to explore through research. Students should find topics that they want to research, apply, and solve. This can then be developed into academic arguments, which counter previous findings on a topic. When evaluating a topic, students can research and explore a topic while using their previous understanding of comparing and contrasting various texts.

With the increased reliance on technology in classrooms, at home, and in all facets of daily life, schools are encouraging use of technology in lessons. Even in the primary grades, teachers are assigning more research-based projects to introduce technology to students at an early age. This way, when students reach higher grade levels, their previous understanding of how and where to find information to answer questions and summarize information can be developed even further. The older grades incorporate the use of multiple sources, asking and evaluating questions, and thinking of their own research topics to explore. This development of instructional strategies and research skills proves to be beneficial in the sciences as well as the new generation of S.T.E.M. learning. Again, reading comprehension skills are essential to the development of research skills.

Addressing Full Range of Learners in the Classroom with Respect to Expository/Informational Texts

Differentiated Instruction Regarding Students with Reading Difficulties

Students struggling with comprehension of expository and informational texts require frequent, smaller group instruction. It is important to review vocabulary, as new vocabulary can be quite difficult. The use of shorter texts, explicit instruction, and repetitive text themes can help struggling readers better understand expository and information texts. Teachers can evaluate struggling students' progress by holding brief discussions with them, as well as giving other informal assessments (including peer think and shares, and oral whole group discussions).

Supporting Students with Special Needs

In addition to re-teaching strategies, special needs students may need more hands-on appropriate activities to increase knowledge and understanding. Games that utilize kinesthetic techniques provide enjoyment, as well as create a learning atmosphere amongst peers. Flash card games that can teach vocabulary or board games with teacher-created questions to support the text can be used.

Addressing the Needs of English Learners and Speakers of Nonstandard English

Language barriers may cause English Language Learners to struggle with understanding text comprehension skills. As language barriers impede comprehension, it is important to break down specific skills and information. Some strategies include flash cards to teach vocabulary, graphic organizers to break information into subgroups, and, if the students are ready, they can write and break down the information with the teacher on their own paper. ELL students' reading skills will advance rapidly with exposure to words and information, as well as the opportunity to apply these skills every day. It is very important to have these students "do" as much as possible, rather than just listen. It is also important to pace these skills and not overload students with too much information.

Addressing the Needs of Advanced Learners

Providing advanced learners with more complex assignments will prevent them from being bored and tuning out. These assignments can be given in a small group led by a teacher or independently, while the teacher works with special needs students or other intervention groups. These assignments should build upon the skill(s) that were addressed that week and should extend current knowledge.

Knowledge in Assessment with Respect to Comprehension of Expository/Informational Texts

Ability to Use Appropriate Formal and Informal Assessments

As mentioned, assessments should be ongoing and frequent. Expository and informational texts tend to be more difficult for students. Therefore, frequent monitoring of comprehension is necessary. Teachers should assess students daily, to ensure they are in an appropriate reading group (based on skill level). Summative assessments should be performed at the end of a lesson or unit and will help the teacher understand what skills have been mastered and what needs to be retaught.

Demonstrating Ability to Analyze Results

Pre-assessments to reading a text may be utilized to understand where the class is as a whole on a given topic. This helps an instructor plan lessons, acknowledge if more exposure on a topic is needed, or evaluate if a more complex assignment can be given if students are already familiar with the topic. Students should be divided into groups based on mastery of the skills that need to be retaught.

Using the Results of Assessments to Plan Effective Instruction

In order for students to be properly placed in appropriate reading groups according to their level, teachers should perform frequent assessments. As students master skills, they will need to be moved into a different group. If students are not assessed daily, they may be receiving instruction that does not progress their skills. Daily assessments can be short and informal. They can be done with whiteboards and questions can be from the text, devised before the lesson, or developed during the lesson. The objective for assessments is to provide teachers with immediate feedback on the day's lesson, and to evaluate if the objectives and standards taught have been met.

Practice Questions

1. What type of texts are considered nonfiction?
    a. Folktales
    b. Memoirs
    c. Fables
    d. Short stories

2. What is a summative assessment?
    a. A formal assessment that is given at the end of a unit of study
    b. An informal assessment that is given at the end of a unit of study
    c. An assessment that is given daily and is usually only a few questions in length, based on the day's objective
    d. An assessment given at the end of the week that is usually based on observation

3. How are typographic features useful when teaching reading comprehension?
    a. Typographic features are graphics used to illustrate the story and help students visualize the text.
    b. Typographic features give the answers in boldfaced print.
    c. Typographic features are not helpful when teaching reading comprehension and should not be used.
    d. Typographic features such as boldface, italics, and subheadings can be used to highlight important vocabulary or content or indicate changes in topics.

4. What do English language learners need to identify prior to comprehending text?
    a. Vocabulary
    b. Figurative language
    c. Author's purpose
    d. Setting

5. What kind of assessment is most beneficial for students with special needs?
    a. Frequent and ongoing
    b. Weekly
    c. Monthly
    d. Summative assessments only at the end of a unit of study

Answer Explanations

1. B: Nonfiction texts include memoirs, biographies, autobiographies, and journalism. Choices *A*, *C*, and *D* are all examples of fictional prose.

2. A: Summative assessments are formal assessments that are given at the end of a unit of study. These assessments are usually longer in length. They are not completed daily. These summative assessments shouldn't be confused with informal assessments, which are used more frequently to determine mastery of the day's objective. However, summative assessments may be used to determine students' mastery in order to form intervention groups thereafter.

3. D: Boldfaced, highlighted, or italicized text notifies a student when a new vocabulary word or idea is present. Subtitles and heading can also alert a student to a change in topic or idea. These features are also important when answering questions, as a student may be able to easily find the answer with these typographic features present.

4. A: English Language Learners should master vocabulary and words in order to fully comprehend text. Figurative language, an author's purpose, and settings are more complex areas and are difficult for English Language Learners. These areas can be addressed once ELL students understand the meanings of words. In order to master comprehension skills, vocabulary and the English language need to be mastered first, but even once vocabulary and English have been mastered, comprehension can still be difficult. Figurative language is culture-based, and inferences may be difficult for those with a different cultural background.

5. A: Assessments should always be frequent and ongoing for all students, but especially for those with special needs. These assessments may be informal but should be given daily after direct instruction and modeling. While summative assessments are important, they should not be the first and only assessment during a unit of study; usually summative assessments come at the end of a unit. Weekly and monthly assessments are too infrequent for remediation, intervention, or identification of struggling areas.

Planning, Organizing, and Managing Reading Instruction Based on Ongoing Assessment

Planning, Organizing, and Managing Standards-Based Reading Instruction

When developing a reading lesson, it is important to demonstrate knowledge of standards in reading instruction. All standards-based programs focus on the educator's ability to interpret and instruct the scope of a text while applying state standards. When creating a lesson, a teacher needs to ensure that their instruction aligns with the use of California SBE adopted materials for instruction and intervention. To ensure that instruction is balanced and comprehensive, instructors should refer to the California Reading/ Language Arts Framework (2014).

To demonstrate the mastery of reading, students should convey their understanding of a text through a written assignment or oral presentation. In order to master the art of writing and presenting, a student needs a complete understanding of the English language and a well-developed vocabulary. Therefore, ELA standards are integrated across the curriculum with reading, writing, speaking, and language skills. These skills are intertwined throughout lessons in order to create a vigorous learning approach. Mastery of this combination of skills demonstrates strong content knowledge and reading comprehension.

The state of California mandates that reading instruction reflect balance. Teachers should use a variety of approaches and strategies to impart knowledge to students. Since students have a variety of learning styles, many approaches should be utilized in the classroom. Students need explicit instruction and modeling by the teacher in order to learn a new skill. Instruction also should provide opportunities for students to demonstrate what they have learned and for them to practice independently.

California advocates that students become career and college ready. In order to do so, students should read a variety of literary and informational texts. Such texts may include pieces extending across a wide variety of genres, timelines, and cultural works. Texts are to be complex and should elicit higher-level thinking skills. For example, literature may include Shakespeare. Similarly, informational text may include the founding documents from the United States.

In alignment with the anchor standards for reading, instructors should ensure that students read closely to determine the meaning of a text. Students should make logical inferences and cite specific evidence when speaking or writing in order to support their conclusions. Students should summarize using key details from the text and analyze why and how authors develop ideas throughout the text. Students should learn how to interpret figurative meanings and analyze how specific phrases and paragraphs relate to each other. They also should assess the point of view and purpose of a text. Oral and written evaluation of similarities and differences amongst a variety of formats is important.

In order to achieve the above skills, students should read and comprehend complex literary and informational text with proficiency. Reading, writing, speaking, listening, and language are skills that are to be interwoven within reading instruction so that students master both written and spoken language. Students should demonstrate the mastery of such skills through written responses to a text that include supporting evidence(s) and citation(s) from the text itself. In addition to writing, students need to perform public speaking projects in order to demonstrate what they have learned from the text.

85

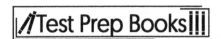

In addition to intertwining several skills, lessons should include a variety of texts. In kindergarten, literature and informational text should be balanced. California state standards for reading indicate that from kindergarten through fifth grade, literary and nonfiction text should reflect a 50/50 balance. Science and social study texts help to build a rich foundation for informational texts. Basal readers are a good source for fiction and nonfiction text. Building a classroom library can provide a variety of both types of texts. In the primary grades, a classroom library can be a primary source of literary text in order to build an interest in reading. Picture books are also a great way to introduce literary text to early readers.

As students approach fifth grade, informational text found in nonfiction novels and basal readers should become more available. From sixth grade to twelfth grade, greater attention is placed on informational text. Informational text should make up 55 percent of a curriculum by the eighth grade and approximately 70 percent of works by the twelfth grade. This is the recommended grade-level distribution of literary and informational passages suggested by the 2009 National Assessment of Educational Progress (NAEP) reading framework. The California state standards adhere to these guidelines and align their instruction with this framework in order to prepare students to become career and college ready.

Teachers will want to include research-based writing lessons of informative, explanatory, and narrative texts. During such lessons, students gather information from multiple sources. Students can use digital media in order to perform such research. This research is used to support claims made in their written responses. Students should address an intended audience in their written work. Additionally, student writing should reflect organization and purpose. Proper citation of the research used within student written responses and technology used to publish work is also important. Published work requires the use of word programs, keyboarding skills, an Internet search engine, and programs such as PowerPoint, Excel, or Google docs.

As for the assessment of speaking and listening, instructors should prepare students to engage in conversation effectively individually or in different-sized groups. Students and instructors may use such discussions as informative assessments to judge students' knowledge of a text. Formative evaluation of students' reading ought to include oral presentations as well. Claims made in such student evaluations ought to be supported with research-based evidence(s) or citations located within the text being discussed.

Students and teachers may use digital media during presentations or assessments in order to allow for more engagement and audience participation. The technology available in the classroom for students and teacher presentations may include projectors and Smart Boards. Many touch-screen boards have replaced chalkboards and whiteboards. These computer-based boards utilize programs that allow students to manipulate material with a stylus or use touchscreen technology. Such manipulation enables students to interact directly with a lesson.

Clickers allow students to choose an answer from a teacher-generated assessment projected on a Smart Board. Implementation of such technology creates an environment where students should be effectively listening to direct instruction in order to respond to the presented questions correctly. Additionally, these types of assessments give teachers immediate data on their students' levels of understanding. Scores from these types of assessments may be linked directly to an electronic gradebook, allowing the teachers an easy way to collect grades. Information collected through such assessments can then be used to create intervention groups.

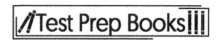

Of course, the use of standard conventions of the English language is important for all the elements of reading and writing. A demonstration of grammar usage throughout assessments is critical. Vocabulary, clarity, and expression should all be used to determine the adequate assessment of a student's response.

Students should respond to reading assessment questions by using evidence from the text—whether that text is informational or literary. In the past, students used personal experience or prior knowledge to respond to questions. Reading lessons and teachers are now using text-dependent questions within assessments. In order to perform well on such assessments, students should be actively engaged in the lesson and text. Students should extract information directly from the source when answering questions and find details based on evidence from the text. Even inferences should be supported by text evidence to support answers. During the evaluation of such assessments, teachers should confirm that an idea was indeed taken from the text itself.

Assessments can be formative or summative. Formative assessments include formal and informal procedures done throughout a unit of study, such as observations, exit tickets, individual whiteboards, or student portfolios. Teachers use formative assessments in order to gauge whether or not additional instruction for a particular skill is required. Summative assessments are usually done at the end of a unit and are considered to be high stakes. Summative assessments are sometimes standardized, which yields a high degree of accuracy in the data. They might also be authentic or task-based, such as a portfolio, which offers teachers a strong understanding of the students' abilities and growth.

Whether formative or summative, assessments should be given frequently and purposefully. This will indicate which students need intervention and which students can be given more independent practice. Frequent assessments help teachers tackle reading difficulties before they become overwhelming. If an instructor waits too long to assess a child, it is more difficult to identify the exact skill with which a student requires intervention. When assessments are given frequently, teachers can readily identify student difficulties in order to provide immediate intervention. This, in turn, increases the chances that a skill is mastered by all students.

Using a systematic approach to reading instruction will help teachers address concerns early on and help them ensure that all students have demonstrated a sufficient level of mastery of particular skills at designated points. Systematic reading approaches should include direct and explicit instruction while giving students opportunities to show what they have learned. Skills should be broken down into smaller units of information in order to allow students to grasp a concept. Such techniques allow students to synthesize smaller concepts into a larger schema. The implementation of mini lessons allows teachers to intervene and give remediation throughout a unit before a larger skill is introduced. In this way, a solid foundation is developed on which students can later build more complex and higher order thinking skills.

In conclusion, instruction should be differentiated to address the variety of learners in the classroom. Instruction should allow for high expectations at each child's learning level. Ongoing assessments will guide an instructor as to which students will benefit from independent practice versus those students who need more remediation.

Key Factors to Consider in Planning Differentiated Reading Instruction

The following are key factors to consider when planning differentiated reading instruction:

- Assess knowledge and skills in the specific area(s) of reading.
- Identify the prerequisite skills that are required for students to benefit from instruction.
- Properly pace the instruction of such skills.
- Understand the complexity of the skills and content that should be presented.
- Provide scaffolding to ensure that all students can access higher-level reading knowledge and skills.

The breakdown of materials and standards over a week is vital. A weeklong reading lesson can be broken down into five sections or days. Skills presented throughout the course of the lesson can be assessed at the end of the week. Teachers can assess student advancement more effectively with smaller group sizes. Therefore, initial assessments should be used to differentiate instruction and to group students according to their abilities and skill levels. Students who have mastered the skill(s) can move on to more complex tasks at a faster pace while working at their seats independently. This gives the instructor time to meet with students who need more remediation and teacher direction. Students who need the most help should meet with the teacher individually for scaffolded remediation of less complex tasks. Struggling students also benefit from slower-paced lessons and additional practice.

The anchor standards for college and career readiness in reading per California state's anchor standards include *key ideas and details*, *craft and structure,* and *integration of knowledge and ideas*:

- Ideas and details: Students must be able to make inferences and draw conclusions from a text, determine central ideas and themes, and analyze how authors develop individuals, events, and ideas throughout the text.

- Craft and structure: Students will need to interpret figurative meanings, analyze how parts of a text relate to each other, and assess points of view.

- Integration of knowledge and ideas: Students must evaluate content across a variety of media and formats.

Managing Differentiated Reading Instruction to Meet the Needs of all Students

The following are ways to organize and manage differentiated reading instruction and interventions to meet the needs of all students:

- Use flexible grouping, individualized instruction, and whole-class instruction as needed.

- Use all components of the core California SBE-adopted materials to make grade-level content accessible for all students.

- Create intervention groups according to the severity of student needs.

Reading instruction begins with daily whole-class lessons that are conducted to introduce new skills. The remaining time of a reading lesson should be dedicated to independent practice for those who have mastered the skill and intervention time for students who are progressing towards the skill.

Lessons should utilize materials adopted by the California School Board of Education (SBE). These materials have been evaluated for consistency with the state's standards and benchmarks. Materials that have been evaluated by California's SBE include textbooks, technology-based resources, curriculum sets, and tests. Thus, there are enough SBE-evaluated materials to use with all types of learners to ensure accessibility for all students.

Students should be assessed during daily lessons. Formative assessments can be done on a daily basis through informal observations. Summative assessments can be done weekly. The teacher ought to use student performance on such assessments to organize the students into smaller intervention groups. The organization of such groups helps to ensure that all students are provided with differentiated interventions on the exact skills in which they struggle. Students who display difficulty in a skill should meet with a teacher for one-on-one or small-group remediation more frequently than students who have mastered the skill. These latter students will be given more independent work at their seats. Groups can be changed accordingly as student performance changes.

Effective Instructional Delivery in Reading as Described in the California RLA Framework (2014)

The following are components of effective instructional delivery in reading:

- Orient students to a new concept through engagement, demonstration, etc.
- Present materials through explicit instruction and modeling.
- Pace instruction of new skills and concepts appropriately.
- Provide students with structured and guided practice that is accompanied with reinforcement, feedback, questions, and peer mediation.
- Provide opportunities for students to apply the skills taught in class through independent practice.

Instruction of all reading skills should include whole-class instruction, orientation, modeling, guided practice, and intervention/independent practice time. Instruction of a skill begins with the teacher modeling the application of the skill with the class as a whole-group activity. Writing the standard that is being taught on the board orients students to the concept/skill that they will be learning during a daily lesson. The written standard serves as a visual aide and reinforces the standard through exposure. The teacher should reference the California state standard before beginning the lesson, throughout the lesson, and at the end of the lesson.

Next, students are to try to apply the skill during guided practice. During guided practice, teachers should provide students with explicit feedback on their performance. Students are to apply the teacher's recommendations as they are made. Such feedback gives students a chance to begin to assess their own understanding of the skill before trying to apply the skill independently.

Formative assessments can be applied during the guided instruction phase of a reading unit. Such assessment can be done through observation and by asking students questions on the particular reading skill(s) that they are practicing. For example, teachers can ask students multiple-choice questions that directly relate to the standard being assessed. By having the students write their answers on individual whiteboards, teachers can quickly observe who responds correctly or incorrectly. In this way, immediate remediation of misconceptions can occur. Additionally, peer mediation and discussion provide open-ended response opportunities for formative assessment of student understanding of a reading or text.

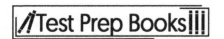

Peer mediation and discussion of texts also give students who have not yet grasped a skill a chance to learn from a peer. At times, students who have mastered a topic can explain a concept to their peers in more age-appropriate language than a teacher can.

After guided instruction, students need time to practice the skill independently or in small performance-based groups. At this time, scaffolding should be provided per individual performance. Data gathered during formative assessments is used in the organization of these performance-based groups. Students who have mastered the skill can work independently. Students who have not yet mastered the skill should work with the teacher in intervention groups.

California content standards suggest three common approaches to providing balanced instruction: the emergent literacy model, the language acquisition model, and the reading readiness model:

- Emergent literacy model: Children are seen to have a natural tendency towards language learning and learn by instinct.

- Language acquisition model: Students possess an instinctual component of literacy development. However, the language acquisition model asserts that language development requires the direct instruction and the employment of sound teaching methods.

- Reading readiness model: Direct instruction is the only way to develop students' literacy skills. This model also states that some students will remain illiterate without receiving the reading skills necessary to gain literacy.

Engaging Students in Reading Instruction

The following are strategies to engage students in reading instruction and motivate them to progress in their reading development:

- Provide instruction that will enable students to develop the skills that are necessary to read successfully.
- Create a stimulating learning environment.
- Provide appropriate, readable, and interesting reading materials.
- Model reading skills by reading aloud to students.
- Encourage parents/guardians to become involved in the development of their students' reading.

Students develop the skills that are needed to read successfully at a faster rate when they enjoy and understand what they are reading. The more children read for pleasure, whether fiction or nonfiction, the more fluent they become in reading. It is much easier to master a test if one understands the content. It is very difficult, if not impossible, for students to comprehend a text if their fluency is consistently being inhibited by the need to phonetically decode the text. Thus, as the fluency of a reader increases, so should their reading comprehension. Therefore, it is important for teachers to offer a wide range of books of various reading levels about topics that are related to the interests of all students in a class. This, in turn, will increase students' ability and motivation to read, strengthen their reading fluency, and increase their reading comprehension.

Creating a comfortable, designated reading area within a classroom helps increase student motivation to read. A reading area should be engaging and inviting. A reading corner can be filled with a variety of texts, furniture for lounging, plants, and décor to produce a stimulating environment. This area can also be embellished with beanbags, lamps, and/or stuffed animals of characters from books with which the students are familiar.

Grouping texts into categories allows students to browse and locate texts that interest them with greater ease. The use of labeled buckets works well for organizing picture books for younger students. Similarly, shelves can be used to organize books by genre for older students. A label maker can be used to label the genre of text located on each shelf. Such organizational methods help students locate what they like to read.

Read-alouds can be used by teachers to model appropriate reading skills. During a read-aloud, students can hear an expressive voice. Through read-alouds, students can make personal connections with a text. Students can then share these connections with their peers. In this way, read-alouds give students an opportunity to interact with and become involved with the text.

Students are more apt to develop reading skills when the skills are reinforced at home. Thus, parents should be encouraged to be involved in the development of their students' reading. Parents can become involved by reading to their children at bedtime or having their children read to them. In doing so, parents reinforce the value of reading for pleasure or purpose in places other than at school.

The library is a great place to interact with adults, parents, and other children while reading. At the library, children can pick from a great variety of books that align with their interests. There are also a lot of libraries that have programs for children and teens. For example, libraries may provide young children with story times, entertaining programs, shows, and clubs. For older teens, libraries may provide book clubs, games, and movie nights. These activities and special events are especially beneficial in encouraging kids to read for pleasure over summer vacation.

Promoting Purposeful Reading of a Wide Variety of Texts

The following are strategies for promoting purposeful and independent reading of a wide variety of texts:

- Promote independent reading of narrative, literary, expository, and informational texts.
- Teach students how to select books that are at appropriate reading levels.
- Use students' personal interests to help motivate them to read independently.
- Provide structured reading opportunities in class.
- Encourage independent reading at home.
- Monitor students' independent reading.

In addition to teacher read-alouds as discussed earlier, students should have approximately twenty minutes per day to read independently. This time should be structured and occur at predictable times throughout the week. Students should be encouraged to read a variety of texts at this time (narrative, literary, expository, and informational texts). Students also should read independently.

In order to benefit from independent reading, students must read texts that are appropriate for their assessed reading level. Therefore, students should be aware of their reading levels and able to select texts that coincide with this level. For students in primary school, the five-finger test can be used in the text-selection process. The five-finger test asserts that if a student has trouble with five or more words on a randomly selected page, then the book is above that student's reading level. For older readers, the teacher can group texts into levels and/or categories, from which students can select based on their personal interests.

In order for independent reading time to be effective, students should be accountable for what is read. A great assessment tool is to have each student give an oral report of one book that they have read during the marking period. Students should be given nightly reading homework as well. Teachers may require students to log the number of minutes read each night. Such reading logs ought to require parents to sign next to the number of minutes a night a child has read.

Creating a Literacy-Rich Environment

Projects and presentations are great ways to create a literacy-rich environment where reading is promoted. Projects and presentations also meet the speaking and writing components of the California Framework for ELA. Additionally, projects and presentations encourage students to use reading and research as an avenue through which they can set and pursue personal goals.

Presentations can include digital and technology components, such as PowerPoint, Glogster, Powtoon, or recorded videos. Projects may be presented as a "grab bag" or tic-tac-toe board that include several options that students can choose to complete. In this way, students can pick projects that meet their individual abilities, goals, and interests. Allowing students to choose from a set group of options also promotes differentiation within a class.

Rather than utilizing reading groups, students can be arranged into book clubs, author studies, literature circles, or other discussion groups. All members of such groups can read the same text together or independently. Either way, the group's members or entire class should come together at some point each week to discuss the selected text.

Support Systems Available to Promote Skillful Teaching of Reading

Professional development (PD) opportunities are often used to expose teachers to strategies that can be used to promote skillful teaching of reading. Sometimes administrators offer incentives for teachers to attend after-school PD courses. Such incentives may include extra pay, credits to advance degrees or salary, or free materials and resources. If money is a factor, schools may be able to receive tuition compensation when teachers take courses that are specific to the schools' goals. Either way, PDs enable teachers to collaborate with coworkers or teachers from other grade levels and/or schools in order to learn from one another.

Grade-level teams and meetings are other ways that teachers can sit down with peers to share materials, ideas, and resources. If students within a grade level are struggling with a particular standard, it is more economical and efficient to address this concern across a grade level. Grade-level teams may be able to order materials with provided funds or grants to enhance their students' learning in reading. There are many resources and books that are directly related to reading state standards and benchmarks. Similarly, workloads can be split up amongst members of the team. Rather than each teacher finding materials for several standards, each member of the team can locate materials for a specific standard with which the majority of the team's students struggle.

Some schools employ a *reading coach* who specializes in ELA and content standards. A primary role of reading coaches is to be trained in reading interventions in order to provide teachers the strategies needed to ensure their students meet annual growth expectations of select benchmarks. In order to become specialists in such reading processes, reading coaches attend district-wide meetings to learn about resources, strategies, and curriculum changes. Reading coaches are great advocates when it comes to getting resources for California SBE materials. They help schools and/or districts select texts, leveled readers, and matching assessments. Reading coaches also train and educate teachers in how to use such resources effectively within their classrooms. Sometimes, reading coaches even teach lessons, help with small groups, or assess students.

Reading Assessments and Best Practices

Three Primary Purposes of Reading Assessment

Performance on reading assessments is indicative of the student's progress in other academic areas as reading is fundamental in all subject areas. Therefore, reading assessments need to be given consistently and analyzed correctly. Data from these assessments should be used to ensure all students are meeting grade-level reading expectations and inform future instruction based on student needs.

Assessment of reading should entail entry-level assessment, progress monitoring, and summative assessment. Each type of assessment is explained below:

Entry-Level Assessment

Entry-level assessments are given before a skill is introduced to determine a student's prior knowledge about the concept. Generally, a teacher can assess a student's prior knowledge of a grade-level subject or skill at the beginning of a week's lesson. Some texts even provide a pre- and post-lesson test. In some cases, schools allow the same test that is to be given at the end of the week to be given at the start of the week prior to learning the skill. Student performance on entry-level assessments is used to determine students' prerequisite knowledge and skills in a particular reading area. In this way, teachers are abler to plan instruction and/or intervention that will most closely meet the needs of all students in a class.

Monitoring of Student Progress

A student's progress in word analysis, fluency, vocabulary, academic language, background knowledge, and comprehension ought to be assessed on an ongoing basis. Ongoing monitoring of student progress is necessary to determine if students are making adequate gains towards the mastery of identified standards or benchmarks.

Progress monitoring can include formal and informal diagnostic assessments. For example, progress monitoring may consist of a brief daily test during a small group intervention or a weekly curriculum-based assessment. Each student's results can be charted and reviewed easily to identify progress (or lack of progress) over time. Student performance data from such assessments should be used to adjust instruction based on students' needs.

Summative Assessment

Summative assessments are administered after a skill has been taught, reinforced, and intervened. Summative assessments are used to determine if students have mastered grade-level standards, benchmarks, or standardized skills. If the summative assessment is open-ended, then it is typically scored by a specific rubric. If the assessment is not open-ended (e.g., a multiple-choice test), then the questions are marked either correct or incorrect.

Students with Individualized Education Programs (IEPs) Who Require Alternative Assessments

The use of more intense assessments and more frequent assessments may be needed for students with IEPs. In order to show progress (or lack of progress), frequent monitoring, daily intervention, and charting of progress and assessments may need to be done. If more than one skill needs to be intervened, a chart and intervention may be needed for each skill. In order to show growth towards grade-level standards and California state standards for reading, these skills should be benchmarked on a weekly basis. Individual intervention and/or small group intervention will need to be accounted for as well.

Quality Indicators that Apply to Standardized Assessments of Reading

The California Standards Tests are used to test for student mastery of state standards. These are considered criterion-referenced tests that demonstrate achievement and performance of the state standards for each student. Both open-ended questions and selected-response items are used to test the standards. Selected-response items cause students to guess but are less time-consuming for students to take. Although open-ended questions take more time to complete and grade, they compel

94

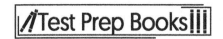
students to use higher-level thinking skills and allow students to demonstrate their understanding of standards authentically.

Standardized tests should be held to a set of quality indicators. These quality indicators are identified and briefly explained below:

- High-order cognitive skills: Approximately one-half of an English standardized test should consist of higher-level thinking skills that require students to transfer and apply their knowledge to a situation.

- High fidelity: Fidelity refers to the critical abilities and authentic applications that an assessment requires from students. Assessments with high fidelity may require research, application, experimentation, evaluation, communication, use of technology, collaboration, or creation.

- Educationally valuable: Standardized assessments should provide teachers with information regarding their students' performance on identified benchmarks or standards. This feedback should be accessible so that it can be used by teachers to inform and guide future instruction.

- Validity, reliability, and fairness: Standardized assessments should be well designed and accurately reflect the standard or benchmark that is being assessed along a continuum of achievement. Standardized assessments should provide evidence that the benchmarks or standards are actually included within the assessment and evidence that such benchmarks or standards are accurately measured. Standardized assessments should be free of cultural, language, socioeconomic, learning style, and special needs biases.

Interpreting Results of Assessments

Student performance from entry-level assessments should be used to identify if students have already mastered a skill before instruction on that skill begins. If all students perform well on questions that pertain to a particular standard or benchmark, then less focus can be given to that standard or benchmark. In this way, more instructional time can be allotted for standards and benchmarks on which students have yet to show mastery.

Observations should be made regularly during progress monitoring and guided practice. Such observations can be recorded in a grade book and referenced in order to determine student gaps in understanding to guide future instruction. During guided practice, the teacher should also provide students with explicit feedback. Students should apply the teacher's recommendations as those recommendations are made. Such feedback gives students a chance to begin to assess their own understanding of the skill; then, the skill is tested through a summative assessment.

Each question on a summative assessment should be linked to a particular standard or benchmark. Student responses per question on standard-aligned summative assessments should be charted and analyzed. In this way, teachers can determine which standards or benchmarks have not yet been mastered by an entire class, a group of students, or an individual. If an entire class responded incorrectly to a question that is in alignment with an identified standard, then that concept needs to be retaught to the entire class. Teachers can also use data gathered from standard-aligned summative assessments to identify which students require remediation or can be advanced within the course of study.

Data from all forms of assessment should be used to form leveled groups. The groups should be dynamic. Thus, as student performance changes, the grouping of students should also change. In this way, all students can be ensured to receive proper intervention of the particular standard(s) or benchmark(s) with which they struggle. This, in turn, increases opportunities for students to master each skillset.

Determining Students' Independent, Instructional, and Frustration Reading Levels

Frequent assessment ensures that students are grouped together according to their ability and their performance on state standards and benchmarks. Thus, different groups may be practicing different skills. Some may be practicing the same skills, but at different paces. Also, some students may need more than one skill retaught. These students may be in more than one intervention group at times.

As small groups work with one another, the teacher should be formatively observing and assessing performance. A teacher should be able to recognize a student's frustration reading level. Heightened frustrations occur when a student cannot understand or pronounce 90 percent of the words in the text. Frustration may also occur when a student cannot answer at least 60 percent of grade-level comprehension questions. A child will not develop reading skills productively at this level. Thus, students performing at this level need additional assistance or may benefit from a higher-leveled text being read aloud to them.

Communicating Assessment Results and Reading Progress

Teachers need to understand school and district policies for communicating results to parents/guardians. If a student has more than one teacher, then it is essential that all of the student's teachers meet and interact regularly. Teachers and parents/guardian need to work together in order to successfully meet the student's needs. Therefore, teachers should have open communication with parents/guardians, especially when a student requires considerable intervention. A teacher should advise the parents/guardians of goals and steps needed to increase the student's achievement.

In order to address student performance, parents/guardians should be provided copies of criterion-referenced tests used by the school and state. These tests include *standards met, standards exceeded*, and *standards in progress*. Such results can be used to discuss student performance during parent/teacher conferences.

Additionally, teachers should keep a reading portfolio for each student. Student reading portfolios may include observations recorded by the teacher, reading tests, projects, formative assessments, or summative assessments. Hard copies should be kept in the portfolio. These copies can be used as a source of reference during parent meetings and/or conferences. Upon request, copies of the originals can be sent home.

For school and district personnel, teachers should keep charts on interventions used and progress on any child who may need or has an IEP. This may be critical when addressing whether the child is eligible for services or the continuation of services.

Practice Questions

1. It is important to choose a variety of texts to elicit higher-level thinking skills. Which of the following text groupings would be appropriate to reach this goal?
   a. Basal readers, fantasy texts, and sci-fi novels
   b. Nonfiction, fiction, cultural pieces, and United States documents
   c. Scholastic magazine articles
   d. Textbooks and high-interest blogs

2. What percentage of informational text should be used in instruction by the time students reach the twelfth grade?
   a. 25 percent
   b. 55 percent
   c. 50 percent
   d. 70 percent

3. The RICA's content is organized into five domains. What is the first domain?
   a. Word analysis and vocabulary based on ongoing assessments
   b. Planning, organizing, and managing math assessment based on ongoing assessments
   c. Comprehension strategies
   d. Planning, organizing, and managing reading instruction based on ongoing assessments

4. A first grader that is in a classroom's reading center appears to be frustrated. How can the teacher best help this student find a book that is at the appropriate reading level?
   a. Have the student do a five-finger test for vocabulary
   b. Pick a new book for the student
   c. Have the student try to figure it out on their own
   d. Have a peer read the book to the student

5. Which element is important for a teacher to consider when planning a lesson?
   a. Pacing
   b. Intervention groups
   c. Modeling and direct instruction
   d. All of the above

Answer Explanations

1. B: California advocates that students become career and college ready. Doing so requires students to read a wide variety of literary and informational texts. Texts may extend across a wide variety of genres, timelines, and cultural works. Nonfiction, fiction, cultural pieces, and United States documents are all excellent examples of texts to use during reading instruction.

2. D: Seventy percent of material students are exposed to during reading instruction should be nonfiction text by the time they reach the twelfth grade. By eighth grade, students should be exposed to 55 percent of nonfiction text. Students should be exposed to a 50/50 balance from kindergarten to fifth grade.

3. D: The California RICA is divided into five domains. The first domain is to understand how to plan, organize, and manage standards-based reading instruction. The other domains include word analysis, fluency, vocabulary, academic language, and background knowledge and comprehension.

4. A: Young students should use the five-finger test to select an appropriate-level text. Using the five-finger test, a student selects a page within a text that they desire to read. The student holds up a finger for each word they are unable to read on that page. If the student has five fingers up after reading the entire page, then the student should stop and choose a book at an easier reading level. If there is not a variety of books of various reading levels from which a student can choose, then the student is likely to become frustrated. Such frustration may cause the student to stop reading for pleasure and see reading as a chore.

5. D: Elements of a good lesson are all of the above criteria. Pacing, modeling, direct instruction, and intervention are necessary to build a strong reading lesson. Teachers need to account for time given by a district for reading. That time should include whole-class instruction of new reading skills. Teachers should then assess students formatively during guided and independent practice in order to break students into groups based on their performance levels.

Writing Tips for Constructed Response Questions

Brainstorm

Don't just start writing! Writing lacks direction if thoughts and ideas aren't organized first. So, before writing a single sentence of the opening paragraph, take a few minutes to **brainstorm**. Write down anything and everything related to the topic. Don't filter out anything, no matter how silly it might seem; it's impossible to know what ideas might grow into a full argument. It might be a good idea to use the scratch paper provided to jot down ideas and organize them, grouping similar ideas together. At this point, keep in mind that the people scoring the test will be looking for variety, creativity, and imagination—in the examples, in the ways the points are made, and especially in the perspectives.

Inventory

Keep brainstorming until the ideas stop flowing (but keep an eye on the clock). Then, take a deep breath, and look at the ideas. An **angle**, or pattern, should start to emerge—a common theme to pull the most promising ideas together. Keep this overarching direction in mind while deciding what to keep and what to drop. Once again, good writing comes from having well-developed and supported ideas, but *great* writing finds a way to connect all those ideas into a single big idea.

Organize

After deciding what written material to use, start putting it all in order. Look for ideas that flow logically. Seek out similarities or differences that draw certain thoughts together into a natural sequence. If one area looks weak or needs more support, either come up with some convincing evidence to strengthen it or take it out. Don't include anything that can't be backed up or that doesn't fit in the flow of the main idea.

Manage the Clock

Don't let the clock be the enemy. By now, it should be possible to see how many points there are and how much time is left. Do some simple math to figure out how much time there is to develop each idea. Don't forget to leave some time to review and proofread the writing.

Write

After all the preparation work is done, writers should have a clear idea of what they want to say. Keep in mind that there are certain things the scorers are looking for to show that the writing is well-thought-out. Also, be sure to write legibly, as the score could be lowered if the handwriting is poor.

Proofread

Everyone makes mistakes in the heat of writing on an exam: a misspelled word, a sentence that doesn't make sense, or a paragraph that seems disjointed and confusing. Be sure to leave a few minutes at the end to go back and reread the writing. Read slowly, trying to hear the words. It may feel silly, but moving the lips will help internalize the flow and make it easier to catch writing problems. Most mistakes are quick fixes, and any writer will be glad to have gone back and corrected them.

Also, be sure to delete any notes left while working through the assignment or any text from the brainstorming session. The formatting (indented paragraphs, for example) should be consistent. Leave readers with a document that looks appealing and "clean"—without mistakes—before they read a single word.

Final Thoughts

When time runs out, it will probably feel like there was room for improvement. That's normal. In fact, scorers understand the difficulties of creating organized, coherent writing in a timed situation under pressure. No one expects the writing to be perfect. With that in mind, here are some ideas for test takers to consider while working through the writing test:

- o **Don't panic**. This is doable. Stop if it feels like brain overload is setting in and drawing a blank is imminent. Take a deep breath and remember the process. Don't force it. It's even okay to stop for a 30-second "mental vacation" to clear the mind.

- o **Make the clock work**. Brainstorming and dividing the task into smaller chunks allows for viewing the remaining time in the least stressful way. If writing an entire essay in 30 minutes is overwhelming, just focus on finishing the next paragraph.

- o **Don't try to impress anyone**. Don't use fancy words just because they're familiar—writers shouldn't use any word that they're not 100 percent sure about. Also, don't add more writing just to make the essay longer. What's important is clear, organized writing. If the ideas have been brainstormed, developed, and written in a logical order, it will be possible to put a lot of meaning into very few words.

Practice Test #1

Word Analysis

1. Structural analysis would be the most appropriate strategy in determining the meaning of which of the following words?
   a. Extra
   b. Improbable
   c. Likely
   d. Wonder

2. A student spells *eagle* as *EGL*. This student is performing at which stage of spelling?
   a. Conventional
   b. Phonetic
   c. Semiphonetic
   d. Transitional

3. Spelling instruction should include which of the following?
   a. Word walls
   b. Daily reading opportunities
   c. Daily writing opportunities
   d. All of the above

4. A kindergarten student is having difficulty distinguishing the letters *b* and *d*. The teacher should do which of the following?
   a. Have the student use a think-aloud to verbalize the directions of the shapes used when writing each letter.
   b. Have the student identify the letters within grade-appropriate texts.
   c. Have the student write each letter five times.
   d. Have the student write a sentence in which all of the letters start with either *b* or *d*.

5. When differentiating phonics instruction for English-language learners (ELLs), teachers should do which of the following?
   a. Increase the rate of instruction.
   b. Begin with the identification of word boundaries.
   c. Focus on syllabication.
   d. Capitalize on the transfer of relevant skills from the learners' original language(s).

6. Which of the following is the most appropriate assessment of spelling for students who are performing at the pre-phonetic stage?
   a. Sight word drills
   b. Phonemic awareness tests
   c. Writing samples
   d. Concepts about print (CAP) test

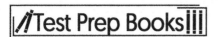

7. Phonological awareness is best assessed through which of the following?
   a. Identification of rimes or onsets within words
   b. Identification of letter-sound correspondences
   c. Comprehension of an audio book
   d. Writing samples

8. The identification of morphemes within words occurs during the instruction of what?
   a. Structural analysis
   b. Syllabic analysis
   c. Phonics
   d. The alphabetic principle

9. Which of the following pairs of words is a homophone?
   a. Playful and replay
   b. To and too
   c. Was and were
   d. Gloomy and sad

10. Nursery rhymes are used in kindergarten to develop what?
    a. Print awareness
    b. Phoneme recognition
    c. Syllabication
    d. Structural analysis

11. High-frequency words such as *be, the*, and *or* are taught during the instruction of what?
    a. Phonics skills
    b. Sight word recognition
    c. Vocabulary development
    d. Structural analysis

12. To thoroughly assess students' phonics skills, teachers should administer assessments that require students to do which of the following?
    a. Decode in context only
    b. Decode in isolation only
    c. Both A and B
    d. Neither A nor B

13. What is a morpheme?
    a. The smallest unit of sound in a language
    b. The sound produced by a single letter
    c. A unit of pronunciation with a single vowel
    d. The smallest meaningful unit of language

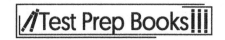

14. A student writes the sentence, "I lik to play soker," instead of, "I like to play soccer." What stage of spelling development has this student reached?
   a. Precommunicative spelling
   b. Semiphonetic spelling
   c. Phonetic spelling
   d. Conventional spelling

15. What is the difference between rhyme and rime?
   a. Rhyme is only used in teaching higher academic concepts in poetry and literature, while rime is an appropriate classroom topic for students of all ages.
   b. Rhyme refers to the repetition of ending sounds (usually the final vowel and consonant) regardless of spelling, while rime depends on both identical spelling and pronunciation.
   c. Rhyme is more applicable to everyday language usage, while rime is only encountered in the classroom.
   d. Rhyme is more effective for developing phonological awareness, while rime is more effective for developing spelling skills.

16. Which of the following is an example of a word with an initial consonant blend?
   a. Frame
   b. Chart
   c. Each
   d. Knife

17. A teacher asks a student, "What sound do you hear at the end of the word 'clock'?" What is the teacher assessing?
   a. The student's ability to apply syllabication
   b. The student's phonological awareness
   c. The student's grasp of the alphabetic principle
   d. The student's conventional spelling skills

18. In order to give students writing practice outside of the classroom, a teacher assigns them to write short journal entries based on their weekend activities. One student writes about her trip to the zoo and includes the following sentence in her journal entry: "I saw bunnys and butterflys at the zoo." Which of the following best explains the student's error?
   a. She has not yet mastered the orthographic rules for -y plurals.
   b. She has not had sufficient independent writing experience.
   c. She has not been exposed to enough reading materials about animals.
   d. She has not seen plurals in written form before; she has only heard them spoken.

19. During a read-aloud assessment, a student reads the word *cooked* with two syllables ("cook-ed"). Which of the following best explains the student's error?
   a. The student is unfamiliar with the content of the text and was unable to decode the word based on background knowledge.
   b. The student has underdeveloped syllabication skills.
   c. The student failed to recognize the inflectional morpheme.
   d. The student was confused because the word contains two different letters that represent the same phoneme, /k/.

103

20. When children begin to negotiate the sounds that make up words in their language independently, what skill(s) are they demonstrating?
    a.   Phonological awareness
    b.   Phonemes
    c.   Phoneme substitution
    d.   Blending

21. What is phonics?
    a.   The study of syllabication
    b.   The study of onsets and rimes
    c.   The study of sound-letter relationships
    d.   The study of graphemes

22. Word analysis skills are NOT critical for the development of what area of literacy?
    a.   Vocabulary
    b.   Reading fluency
    c.   Spelling
    d.   Articulation

23. How do the majority of high-frequency sight words differ from decodable words?
    a.   They do not rhyme.
    b.   They do not follow the alphabetic principle.
    c.   They do not contain onsets.
    d.   They contain rimes.

24. What developmental stage of writing are children demonstrating when they begin to leave spaces between words with a mixture of uppercase and lowercase letters?
    a.   Emergence of beginning sound
    b.   Strings of letters
    c.   Words represented by consonants
    d.   Transitional phase

25. When a student looks at a word and is able to tell the teacher that the letters spell C-A-T, but the student cannot actually say the word, what is the spelling stage of the student?
    a.   Alphabetic Spelling
    b.   Within Word Pattern Spelling
    c.   Derivational Relations Spelling
    d.   Emergent Spelling

26. A student is trying to read the word preferred. She first recognizes the word red at the end, then sounds out the rest of the word by breaking it down into "pre," then "fer," then "red." Finally she puts it together and says "preferred." This student is displaying what attribute?
    a.   Phonemic awareness
    b.   Phonics
    c.   Fluency
    d.   Vocabulary

27. What allows readers to effectively translate print into recognizable speech?

104

a. Fluency
b. Spelling
c. Phonics
d. Word decoding

Constructed Response

Instructions: Prepare an organized written response to the following topic. Your response should be 150 to 300 words.

Scenario: Elementary school students were assigned Chromebooks at the beginning of the year, which they use to research information and watch educational videos about various subject areas, like Biology and History. Some of the students struggle with reading comprehension, and their teacher would like them to practice word analysis with their Chromebooks.

Task 1: Provide a definition of word analysis discuss how it can simplify student understanding of content area material.

Task 2: Discuss how word analysis can be facilitated through technology (such as Chromebooks).

Fluency

1. What are the three interconnected indicators of reading fluency?
    a. Phonetics, word morphology, and listening comprehension
    b. Accuracy, rate, and prosody
    c. Syntax, semantics, and vocabulary
    d. Word exposure, phonetics, and decodable skills

2. Which isn't true of effective independent reading?
    a. Students should read texts that are below their reading levels during independent reading.
    b. Students need to demonstrate fluency before reading independently.
    c. Students who don't yet display automaticity should whisper to themselves when reading aloud.
    d. Students who demonstrate automaticity in decoding should be held accountable during independent reading.

3. Timed oral reading can be used to assess which of the following?
    a. Phonics
    b. Listening comprehension
    c. Reading rate
    d. Background knowledge

4. Syntax is best described as what?
    a. The arrangement of words into sentences
    b. The study of language meaning
    c. The study of grammar and language structure
    d. The proper formatting of a written text

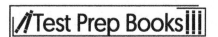

5. What do informal reading assessments allow that standardized reading assessments don't allow?
   a. The application of grade-level norms toward a student's reading proficiency
   b. The personalization of reading assessments in order to differentiate instruction
   c. The avoidance of partialities in the interpretation of reading assessments
   d. The comparison of an individual's reading performance to that of other students in the class

6. When building a class library, a teacher should be cognizant of the importance of what?
   a. Providing fiction that contains concepts relating to the background knowledge of all students in the class.
   b. Utilizing only nonfiction text that correlates to state and national standards in order to reinforce academic concept knowledge.
   c. Utilizing a single genre of text in order to reduce confusion of written structures.
   d. Including a wide range of fiction and nonfiction texts at multiple reading levels.

7. Samantha is in second grade and struggles with fluency. Which of the following strategies is likely to be most effective in improving Samantha's reading fluency?
   a. The teacher prompts Samantha when she pauses upon coming across an unknown word.
   b. The teacher records Samantha as she reads aloud.
   c. The teacher reads a passage out loud several times to Samantha and then has Samantha read the same passage.
   d. The teacher uses read-alouds and verbalizes contextual strategies that can be used to identify unfamiliar words.

8. Reading fluency is best described as the ability to do what?
   a. Read smoothly and accurately
   b. Comprehend what is read
   c. Demonstrate phonetic awareness
   d. Properly pronounce a list of words

Constructed Response

Instructions: Prepare an organized written response to the following topic. Your response should be 75 to 125 words.

Scenario: Mr. Brown is a reading specialist at Carroll High School and assists several teachers and classes with literacy development skills. While most students seem to be writing well, Mr. Brown notices that several students in the classes seem to have trouble reading written words. These children come from a wide range of backgrounds, including native and non-native English speakers.

Task: Describe how Mr. Brown can guide the instructors in addressing the reading issues with differentiated instruction.

Vocabulary, Academic Language, and Background Knowledge

1. Context clues assist vocabulary development by providing what?
   a. A knowledge of roots, prefixes, and suffixes that are used to determine the meaning of a word
   b. Information within the sentence that surrounds an unknown word and is used to determine the word's meaning
   c. Content learned in previous grades that serves as a bridge to the new term
   d. Background knowledge to fill in a missing word within a sentence

2. What can be used when a student comes across an unfamiliar word?
   a. Decoding skills
   b. Structural analysis
   c. Contextual clues
   d. Any of the above

3. A teacher writes a morpheme and its definition in the center of a word map, such as that displayed below.

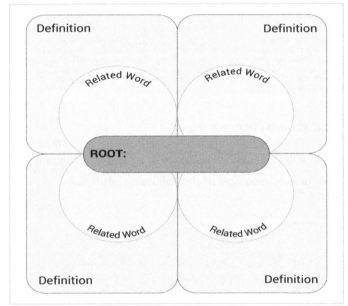

He then asks students to think of other English words that also contain the given morpheme. This activity is most likely to promote students' vocabulary development by helping them to do what?
   a. Apply concept mapping to show similarities and differences amongst a group of words
   b. Gain exposure to common affixes
   c. Determine the meaning of unknown words that contain a known morpheme
   d. Use phonics to determine the meaning of unknown word

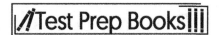
4. A student writes the following in an essay:

   Protestors filled the streets of the city. Because they were dissatisfied with the government's leadership.

Which of the following is an appropriately punctuated correction for this sentence?
   a. Protestors filled the streets of the city, because they were dissatisfied with the government's leadership.
   b. Protesters, filled the streets of the city, because they were dissatisfied with the government's leadership.
   c. Because they were dissatisfied with the government's leadership protestors filled the streets of the city.
   d. Protestors filled the streets of the city because they were dissatisfied with the government's leadership.

5. While studying vocabulary, a student notices that the words *circumference*, *circumnavigate*, and *circumstance* all begin with the prefix *circum–*. The student uses her knowledge of affixes to infer that all of these words share what related meaning?
   a. Around, surrounding
   b. Travel, transport
   c. Size, measurement
   d. Area, location

6. A student wants to rewrite the following sentence:

   Entrepreneurs use their ideas to make money.

He wants to use the word *money* as a verb, but he isn't sure which word ending to use. What is the appropriate suffix to add to *money* to complete the following sentence?

   Entrepreneurs _____ their ideas.

   a. –ize
   b. –ical
   c. –en
   d. –ful

7. A student reads the following sentence:

   A hundred years ago, automobiles were rare, but now cars are ubiquitous.

However, she doesn't know what the word *ubiquitous* means. Which key context clue is essential to decipher the word's meaning?

   a. Ago
   b. Cars
   c. Now
   d. Rare

108

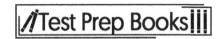

8. A local newspaper is looking for writers for a student column. A student would like to submit his article to the newspaper, but he isn't sure how to format his article according to journalistic standards. What resource should he use?
    a. A thesaurus
    b. A dictionary
    c. A style guide
    d. A grammar book

9. A student encounters the word *aficionado* and wants to learn more about it. It doesn't sound like other English words he knows, so the student is curious to identify the word's origin. What resource should he consult?
    a. A thesaurus
    b. A dictionary
    c. A style guide
    d. A grammar book

10. Which domain is likely to be used by a website run by a nonprofit group?
    a. .com
    b. .edu
    c. .org
    d. .gov

11. The following is an example of what type of sentence?
    Although I wished it were summer, I accepted the change of seasons, and I started to appreciate the fall.

    a. Compound
    b. Simple
    c. Complex
    d. Compound-complex

12. Read the following passage to answer the question below:
    The teacher directed the children's attention to the diagram, but the children couldn't understand the information.

This is an example of what type of sentence?
    a. Complex
    b. Compound
    c. Simple
    d. Compound-complex

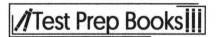

13. Read the following sentences to answer the question below:
Give me a shout back when you can.

Please return my call at your earliest convenience.

What is the main difference in these two sentences?
a. Point of view
b. Dialect
c. Accent
d. Register

14. What are the three tiers of vocabulary?
a. Conversational, academic, and domain-specific language
b. Informal, formal, and academic
c. Social, professional, and academic
d. Phonics, fluency, and rate

15. A teacher asks a student to describe a beautiful day. The student says the flowers were pretty, the air was warm, and animals were running. The teacher asks the student to specify how many flowers there were—just a few hopeful buds or an abundance of blossoms? Was the air still or breezy? How did it feel? The teacher is developing which trait in the student?
a. Voice
b. Word choice
c. Organization
d. Presentation

16. Writing practice for the sole purpose of communicating refers to what kind of writing?
a. Persuasive
b. Informational
c. Narrative
d. Purposeful

17. Speaking, listening, reading, and writing are four essential elements of what?
a. Developmentally appropriate practice
b. The Abecedarian Approach
c. Literacy development
d. Task, purpose, and audience

18. Synonyms, antonyms, and homonyms are examples of what?
a. Syntax relationships
b. Pragmatic relationships
c. Semantic relationships
d. Morphology relationships

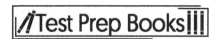
19. Several generations ago, immigrants and locals in a region developed a simplified mixture of their two languages in order to carry out basic communication tasks. However, usage of this mixed language increased, and later generations passed it down to their children as their first language. These children are now speaking what kind of language?

    a. A pidgin
    b. A Creole
    c. A jargon
    d. A regionalism

Constructed Response

Instructions: Prepare an organized written response to the following topic. Your response should be 75 to 125 words.

Scenario: Teachers in an elementary school want to focus on the role of vocabulary in improving reading comprehension. They decide to target students' vocabularies by using a variety of strategies, including the cultivation of literacy-rich environments.

Task 1: Explain how teachers and administrators can involve students in the process of creating and cultivating literacy-rich environments.

Task 2: Briefly outline how literacy-rich environments can help to improve vocabulary and reading comprehension in students.

Comprehension

1. Which is NOT a reason why independent reading is important for developing reading comprehension?

    a. It helps students develop a lifelong love of reading.
    b. It encourages students to read a genre they enjoy.
    c. It provides an opportunity for students to read at their own pace.
    d. It gives students time to visit the reading corner, which is an area of the classroom that is restful and enjoyable.

2. Why are purposeful read-alouds by a teacher important to enhance reading comprehension?

    a. They encourage students to unwind from a long day and reading lesson.
    b. They encourage students to listen for emphasis and tone.
    c. They encourage students to compare the author's purpose to the teacher's objective.
    d. They encourage students to work on important work from earlier in the day while listening to a story.

3. Which of the following is the study of what words mean in certain situations?

    a. Morphology
    b. Pragmatics
    c. Syntax
    d. Semantics

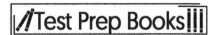

4. What is "text evidence" when referring to answering a comprehension question?
  a. Taking phrases directly from the text itself to answer a question
  b. Using a variety of resources to find the answer
  c. Using technology and websites to locate an answer
  d. Paraphrasing and using a student's own words to answer the question

5. The RICA for reading comprehension addresses which three of the listed comprehension areas?
  a. Objective, subjective, and inferential comprehension
  b. Nonfiction, fiction, and objective comprehension
  c. Literal, inferential, and evaluative comprehension
  d. Literal, inferential, subjective comprehension

6. Why are group-based discussion MOST important in the classroom to enhance reading comprehension (e.g., think pair share)?
  a. They promote student discussions without the teacher present.
  b. They promote student discussions with a friend.
  c. They promote student discussions so that those who didn't understand the text can get answers from another student.
  d. They give all students a voice and allow them to share their answers, rather than one student sharing an answer with the class.

7. Which of the following is NOT useful when initially helping students understand and comprehend a piece of text?
  a. Graphic organizers
  b. Note-taking
  c. Small intervention groups
  d. Extension projects and papers

8. Why are intervention groups important to advanced learners?
  a. They are not useful, as they do not need intervention in a particular skill.
  b. They can be used to teach struggling students.
  c. They can be given more advanced and complex work.
  d. They can be given tasks to do in the classroom while others are meeting for intervention.

9. Which of the following can be useful when working with intervention groups of struggling readers?
  a. Having the teacher read aloud a text to the students while they take notes
  b. Having students read the text silently
  c. Give independent work and explaining the directions in detail before they take it back to their seat
  d. Providing games for them to play while the teacher observes

10. What should be taught and mastered first when teaching reading comprehension?
  a. Theme
  b. Word analysis and fluency
  c. Text evidence
  d. Writing

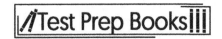

11. What is the method of categorizing text by its structure and literary elements called?
a. Fiction
b. Nonfiction
c. Genre
d. Plot

12. A reader is distracted from following a story because she is having trouble understanding why a character has decided to cut school, so the reader jumps to the next page to find out where the character is headed. This is an example of what?
a. Self-monitoring comprehension
b. KWL charts
c. Metacognitive skills
d. Directed reading-thinking activities

13. A class silently reads a passage on the American Revolution. Once they are done, the teacher asks the students to name the two sides who were fighting, the reason they were fighting, and the winner. What skill is the teacher gauging?
a. Orthographic development
b. Fluency
c. Comprehension
d. Phonics

14. Which trait is most commonly associated with giving individuality and style to writing?
a. Voice
b. Word choice
c. Presentation
d. Ideas

15. Which mode of writing aims to inform the reader objectively about a particular subject or idea and typically contains definitions, instructions, or facts within its subject matter?
a. Argumentative
b. Informative
c. Narrative
d. Descriptive

16. Editorials, letters of recommendation, and cover letters most likely incorporate which writing mode?
a. Argumentative
b. Informative
c. Narrative
d. Descriptive

Constructed Response

Instructions: Prepare an organized written response to the following topic. Your response should be 150 to 300 words.

Scenario: The teachers in an elementary school are proactively trying to implement content-area reading instruction in their classrooms. Their goal is to better their students' writing skills and increase

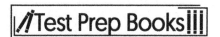

comprehension and writing fluency. However, their budget is low, and the implementation must be cost-effective.

Task 1: Briefly provide an example of content-area reading instruction and describe the process in full detail while aligning the process with the budget constraints.

Task 2: Talk about how this instruction will align with an increase in comprehension and writing fluency for the entire school.

Planning, Organizing, and Managing Reading Instruction Based on Ongoing Assessment

1. What is an effective strategy when working with a child who has an Individualized Education Program (IEP)?
    a. Provide remediation during which the teacher works with the student on a particular skill
    b. Allow the student to work independently
    c. Chart the student's performance on a particular skill on a weekly basis in order to observe the student's growth over time
    d. A and C only

2. Which best describes the areas included in the California English Language standards for reading instruction?
    a. Writing, language, speaking, and reading
    b. Reading and writing only
    c. Speaking and reading only
    d. Language development and reading only

3. What is the goal of a reading specialist position at a school site?
    a. To inform staff of changes in the curriculum
    b. To offer reading lessons in the classroom
    c. To instruct staff on how to do their job
    d. A and B only

4. Which of the following is the best way to utilize a reading center or corner in a classroom?
    a. As a spot for students to play games
    b. As a private and quiet place to chat about books
    c. As a location to provide a variety of leveled readers
    d. As fun and entertaining décor to enhance a comfortable learning environment

5. Which of the following is a guideline of reading instruction in California?
    a. Instruction should be templated.
    b. Instruction should be differentiated.
    c. Instruction should be offered without prior modeling.
    d. Instruction should be the same for each student.

6. What types of questions should be offered in an assessment in order to check for its validity?
   a. Open-ended questions only
   b. Selected-response questions
   c. Both open-ended questions and multiple-choice questions
   d. None of these

7. Which is NOT a component of an effective reading lesson?
   a. Presentation
   b. Guided Practice
   c. Modeling
   d. Research

8. If the majority of students in the classroom did not master a skill, what is the next step that a teacher should take?
   a. Reteach the skill to the entire class
   b. Break the class into smaller groups to remediate the skill
   c. Have students mediate with each other about the skill
   d. Move on to the next skill because time is critical

9. What nonfiction texts can be used to teach reading standards?
   a. United States documents
   b. Magazines for pleasure
   c. Science and social studies textbooks
   d. A and C only

10. When selecting and organizing intervention groups, which of the following is most important?
    a. Organize students according to level
    b. Organize students according to grades on their prior report cards
    c. Organize students according to the opinions of the students' previous teachers
    d. Organize according to student behavior in the classroom

11. A student has quickly written a story and turned it in without reading it. To help reinforce the POWER strategy, the teacher tells the student go back and read his story. This POWER stage is called what?
    a. Prewriting
    b. Evaluating
    c. Organizing
    d. Revising

12. During which stage of the POWER strategy are graphic organizers used?
    a. Pre-writing
    b. Organizing
    c. Writing
    d. Evaluating

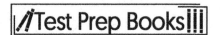

13. A teacher wants his students to write a story over two weeks. They are instructed to write a draft the first day. On each of the following days, he asks the students to develop and edit the story for one of the following: ideas, organization, voice, word choice, sentence fluency, conventions, and presentation. What does this teaching technique incorporate?
    a. Ideas
    b. POWER strategy
    c. Cross-curricular integration
    d. 6+1 Traits

14. In the 6+1 Traits model, which trait teaches students to build the framework of their writing?
    a. Conventions
    b. Word choice
    c. Ideas
    d. Organization

15. In the 6+1 Traits model, which trait ultimately forms the content of the writing?
    a. Conventions
    b. Word choice
    c. Ideas
    d. Voice

16. Rating scales, student logs, and the POWER method are effective assessment practices for what area of literacy development?
    a. Reading
    b. Writing
    c. Spelling
    d. Listening

17. Volume, articulation, and awareness of audience help with what practice?
    a. Effective instruction
    b. Communication
    c. Active listening
    d. Oral presentations

18. Offering a presenter with undivided attention and asking relevant and timely questions are examples of what skill set?
    a. Active listening skills
    b. Effective speaking
    c. Formal communication
    d. Informal communication

19. What is the method called that teachers use before and after reading to improve critical thinking and comprehension?
    a. Self-monitoring comprehension
    b. KWL charts
    c. Metacognitive skills
    d. Directed reading-thinking activities

20. When a student looks back at a previous reading section for information, he or she is using which of the following?
    a. Self-monitoring comprehension
    b. KWL charts
    c. Metacognitive skills
    d. Directed reading-thinking activities

21. Which choice of skills is NOT part of Bloom's Taxonomy?
    a. Remembering and understanding
    b. Applying and analyzing
    c. Listening and speaking
    d. Evaluating and creating

22. Predicting, summarizing, questioning, and clarifying are steps of what?
    a. Reciprocal teaching
    b. Comprehensive teaching
    c. Activation teaching
    d. Summative teaching

23. When a student asks, "What do I know?" "What do I want to know?" and "What have I learned?" and records the answers in a table, he or she is using which of the following?
    a. Self-monitoring comprehension
    b. KWL charts
    c. Metacognitive skills
    d. Directed reading-thinking activities

24. Phonemic awareness, phonics, fluency, vocabulary, and comprehension are the five basic elements of what?
    a. Bloom's Taxonomy
    b. Spelling instruction
    c. Reading education
    d. Genre

25. A teacher wants to help her students write a nonfiction essay on how the Pueblos built their homes. Before they write, she helps the students make clay from cornstarch and water, draw a plan for the house with a ruler, and build it using the clay and leaves from the schoolyard. These exercises are examples of what?
    a. Proficiency
    b. Collaboration
    c. Constructive writing
    d. Cross-curricular integration

Constructed Response: Case Study

Instructions: Prepare an organized written response to a case study of an elementary student. Your response should be 300 to 600 words and address information pertinent to each of the five domains.

Scenario: The following case study is focused on Caleb, a second-grade student. Caleb's primary instructor has noticed that when Caleb reads material aloud in class, he will often take long pauses and

117

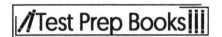

read the sentences slower than the other students. This sometimes causes him to stutter or hesitate during longer sentences. Another issue is that sometimes he will switch the order of the words he sees, for example, putting the word *the* after the word *cat* in a sentence. Despite this, Caleb is very bright and seems to fully grasp the context of the material. He also appears to be engaged when answering questions but is hesitant when having to read in front of the class.

Caleb's teacher has requested that Mr. Breiner, the reading specialist, evaluate Caleb to understand what might be causing his issues. While Caleb is highly intelligent, the teacher is wondering whether his problems with reading may indicate a reading disorder. Mr. Breiner has been requested to present ideas on how to help Caleb's reading skills improve. The teacher wants to be able to learn how to address reading issues like Caleb's in the future, or at least be able to identify core literary issues very early in the developmental stage.

Using the information in the scenario and the notes below, respond to each of the tasks in a way that displays your understanding of literacy assessment and instructional strategies.

Teacher notes:

- When reading the sentence, "The next-door neighbors adopted the cat that had been homeless," Caleb switched *the* and *cat*. He also seemed to take longer to sound out *homeless*.

- Longer sentences seem to cause Caleb confusion when reading aloud.

- In some of his writing responses, Caleb will sometimes switch the letters within the words or the words themselves.

- Caleb understands material clearly and gives insightful thoughts aloud. No speech problems were observed.

Your response should completely address the following tasks:

Task 1: Identify methods of observation that may indicate whether or not Caleb has a learning disorder. What kind of assessments can be used to determine if his reading difficulties are tied to specific written English structures or if his pausing indicates other psychological disconnects?

Task 2: Based on Caleb's reading difficulties, what are some teaching strategies that can be used to help him improve? Provide details on why differentiating Caleb's instruction would be a major step in bolstering his reading ability.

Answer Explanations #1

Word Analysis

1. B: Structural analysis focuses on the meaning of morphemes. Morphemes include base words, prefixes, and word endings (inflections and suffixes) that are found within longer words. Students can use structural analysis skill to find familiar word parts within an unfamiliar word in order to decode the word and determine the definition of the new word. The prefix *im-* (meaning not) in the word *improbable* can help students derive the definition of an event that is not likely to occur.

2. B: The student is performing at the phonetic stage. Phonetic spellers will spell a word as it sounds. The speller perceives and represents all of the phonemes in a word. However, because phonetic spellers have limited sight word vocabulary, irregular words are often spelled incorrectly.

3. D: All of the above. The creation of word walls, Choice *A*, is advantageous during the phonetic stage of spelling development. On a word wall, words that share common consonant-vowel patterns or letter clusters are written in groups. Choices *B* and *C*, daily reading and writing opportunities, are also important in spelling instructions. Students need daily opportunities in order to review and practice spelling development. Daily journals or exit tickets are cognitive writing strategies effective in helping students reflect on what they have learned.

4. A: The teacher should have the student use a think-aloud to verbalize the directions of the shapes used when writing each letter. During think-alouds, teachers voice the metacognitive process that occurs when writing each part of a given letter. Students should be encouraged to do likewise when practicing writing the letters.

5. D: Teachers should capitalize on the transfer of relevant skills from the learner's original language(s). In this way, extra attention and instructional emphasis can be applied toward the teaching of sounds and meanings of words that are nontransferable between the two languages.

6. C: Writing samples. During this stage, students participate in pre-communicative writing, which appears to be a jumble of letter-like forms rather than a series of discrete letters. Samples of students' pre-communicative writing can be used to assess their understanding of the alphabetic principle and their knowledge of letter-sound correspondences.

7. A: Identification of rimes or onsets within words. Instruction of phonological awareness includes detecting and identifying word boundaries, onsets/rimes, syllables, and rhyming words.

8. A: Structural analysis. Structural analysis is a word recognition skill that focuses on the meanings of word parts, or morphemes, during the introduction of a new word. Choice *B*, syllabic analysis, is a word analysis skill that helps students split words into syllables. Choice *C*, phonics, is the direct correspondence between and blending of letters and sounds. Choice *D*, the alphabetic principle, teaches that letters or other characters represent sounds.

9. B: Homophones are words that are pronounced the same way but differ in meaning and/or spelling. To and too are homophones because they are pronounced the same way but differ in both meaning and spelling. Choices *A*, *C*, and *D* are not homophones because they do not sound the same when spoken aloud.

10. B: Nursery rhymes are used in kindergarten to develop phoneme recognition. Rhyming words are often almost identical except for their beginning letter(s), so rhyming is a great strategy to implement during the analytic phase of phoneme development.

11. B: Sight word recognition. Sight words, sometimes referred to as high-frequency words, are words that are used often but may not follow the regular principles of phonics. Sight words may also be defined as words that students are able to recognize and read without having to sound out.

12. C: Decoding should be assessed in context in addition to isolation. To assess in context, students read passages from appropriate texts aloud to the teacher so that the teacher can analyze their approach to figuring out unknown words. Decoding should also be assessed in isolation. In these types of assessments, students are given a list of words and/or phonics patterns. Initially, high-frequency words that follow predictable phonics patterns are presented. The words that are presented become more challenging as a student masters less difficult words.

13. D: The smallest meaningful unit of language. A morpheme is the smallest unit of language that still contains meaning and cannot be broken down further. A word may be a single morpheme or several morphemes. For example, the word *horse* is a single morpheme, but the word *horseback* consists of two morphemes. The smallest unit of sound, Choice *A*, in a language is a phoneme, and a unit of pronunciation with a single vowel, Choice *C*, is a syllable, so those answers are incorrect.

14. C: The student's spelling demonstrates phonetic awareness, or the understanding that letters correlate to produced sounds. In precommunicative spelling, Choice *A*, a student may know how to write some letters but has not grasped how they correspond to sounds. As students develop their phonetic awareness, they begin using single letters (for example, *u* instead of *you*) and other simplified spellings. A student at the phonetic stage, Choice *C*, such as this recognizes, for example, that the letter *k* represents the phoneme /k/ and has used it to spell the word *soccer*. At the conventional spelling stage, Choice *D*, students are able to use correct spellings even when they do not follow standard phonetic rules.

15. B: Rhyme refers to the repetition of ending sounds (usually the final vowel and consonant) regardless of spelling, while rime depends on both identical spelling and pronunciation. Both rhyme and rime refer to the repetition of ending sounds, and both are useful in teaching word recognition, pronunciation, and orthographic patterns. However, words with ending rhymes may sound the same but use different spelling (for example, *tough* and *stuff*), whereas rimes will always have identical spelling (*stop* and *pop* or *song* and *long*).

16. A: A consonant blend occurs when two or more consonants are placed together to produce a combined pronunciation, but each individual consonant sound can still be heard. Therefore, the word *frame* contains a consonant blend. *Chart*, Choice *B*, and *knife*, Choice *D*, are not correct answers because, while each word does begin with two consonants, they are examples of digraphs, or combinations of two letters that create one new sound (that is, the *kn* in *knife* produces a single sound and is not pronounced with the individual phonemes /k/ and /n/). *Each*, Choice *C*, is not correct because it begins with a diphthong, or two vowels that combine into a single syllable.

17. B: The teacher is asking the student to isolate a single sound, or phoneme, in the context of a word. The understanding that words are made up of individual sounds is phonological awareness. Choice *A* is incorrect because syllabication is the division of words into syllables, or units of pronunciation with a

120

single vowel sound. Choice *C* is incorrect because the alphabetic principle is the understanding that letters (or graphemes) represent sounds (or phonemes); in this example, the teacher is asking the student to listen to a word rather than recognize it visually. Choice *D* is incorrect for the same reason.

18. A: She has not yet mastered the orthographic rules for -*y* plurals. Orthographic rules govern spelling conventions—in this case, the rule that words ending with -*y* preceded by a consonant change to an -*ies* ending in the plural form. She may have encountered such words in writing before, but she has not formalized the rule in her own writing yet.

19. C: The student failed to recognize the inflectional morpheme. An inflectional morpheme is one that changes the word form or tense, such as -*es* at the end of some plurals or, in this case, -*ed* for past tense. Because inflectional morphemes can affect pronunciation (for example, the name *Ed* is pronounced different from the past tense -*ed* found in *cooked*), failure to recognize them can lead to pronunciation errors such as the one in this example.

20. A: Phonological awareness refers to a child's ability to understand and use familiar sounds in their social environment in order to form coherent words. Phonemes are defined as distinct sound units in any given language. Phonemic substitution refers to the ability to substitute specific phonemes for others. Blending refers to the ability to construct or build words from individual phonemes by blending the sounds together in a unique sequence.

21. C: When children begin to recognize and apply sound-letter relationships independently and accurately, they are demonstrating a growing mastery of phonics. Phonics is the most commonly used method for teaching people to read and write by associating sounds with their corresponding letters or groups of letters, using a language's alphabetic writing system. Syllabication refers to the ability to break down words into their individual syllables. The study of onsets and rimes strives to help students recognize and separate a word's beginning consonant or consonant-cluster sound, the onset, from the word's rime, the vowel and/or consonants that follow the onset. A grapheme is a letter or a group of letters in a language that represent a sound.

22. D: Breaking down words into their individual parts, studying prefixes, suffixes, root words, rimes, and onsets are all examples of word analysis. When children analyze words, they develop their vocabulary and strengthen their spelling and reading fluency.

23. B: Although some high-frequency sight words are decodable, the majority of them are not. This means they do not follow the Alphabetic Principle, which relies on specific letter-sound correspondence. High-frequency sight words appear often in children's literature and are studied and memorized in order to strengthen a child's spelling and reading fluency. High-frequency sight words, as well as decodable words, may or may not rhyme and may or may not contain onsets and rimes.

24. C: There are eight developmental writing stages:

- Scribbling
- Letter-like symbols
- Strings of letters
- The emergence of beginning sounds
- Words represented by consonants
- Initial, middle, and final sounds

121

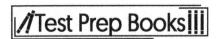
- Transitional phase
- Standard spelling

When children begin to leave visible spacing between words, even if those words are incorrectly spelled or if there is a mixture of upper- and lower-case letters, they are considered to be at the *Words represented by consonants* stage.

25. D: During the Emergent Spelling stage, children can identify letters but not the corresponding sounds. The other choices are all fictitious.

26. B: Phonics is the ability to apply letter-sound relationships and letter patterns in order to accurately pronounce written words. Phonemic awareness is the understanding that words are comprised of a combination of sounds. Fluency is an automatic recognition and accurate interpretation of text. Vocabulary is the body of words known to a person.

27. C: Phonics allows readers to effectively translate print into recognizable speech. If children lack proficiency in phonics, their ability to read fluently and to increase vocabulary will be limited.

Fluency

1. B: According to substandard 2 of RICA's Competency 8 Content Specification, key indicators of reading fluency include accuracy, rate, and prosody. Phonetics and decodable skills aid fluency. Syntax, semantics, word morphology, listening comprehension, and word exposure aid vocabulary development.

2. A: Once students become fluent readers, independent reading can begin. Students who don't yet display automaticity may need to read out loud or whisper to themselves during independent reading time. Independent silent reading accompanied by comprehension accountability is an appropriate strategy for students who demonstrate automaticity in their decoding skills. Also, each student should be provided with a text that matches their reading level.

3. C: The most common measurement of reading rate includes the oral contextual timed readings of students. During a timed reading, the number of errors made within a given amount of time is recorded. This data can be used to identify if a student's rate is improving and if the rate falls within the recommended range for his or her grade level.

4. A: Syntax refers to the arrangement of words and phrases to form well-developed sentences and paragraphs. Semantics has to do with language meaning. Grammar is a composite of all systems and structures utilized within a language and includes syntax, word morphology, semantics, and phonology. Cohesion and coherence of oral and written language are promoted through a full understanding of syntax, semantics, and grammar.

5. B: Informal reading assessments allow teachers to create differentiated assessments that target reading skills of individual students. In this way, teachers can gain insight into a student's reading strengths and weaknesses. Informal assessments can help teachers decide what content and strategies need to be targeted. However, standardized reading assessments provide all students with the same structure to assess multiple skills at one time. Standardized reading assessments cannot be individualized. Such assessments are best used for gaining an overview of student reading abilities.

6. D: Students within a single classroom come with varied background knowledge, interests, and needs. Thus, it's unrealistic to find texts that apply to all. Students benefit when a wide range of fiction and nonfiction texts are available in a variety of genres, promoting differentiated instruction.

7. D: This answer alludes to both read-alouds and think-alouds. Modeling fluency can be done through read-alouds. Proper pace, phrasing, and expression of text can be modeled when teachers read aloud to their students. During think-alouds, teachers verbalize their thought processes when orally reading a selection. Teachers' explanations may describe strategies they use as they read to monitor their comprehension. In this way, teachers explicitly model the metacognition processes that good readers use to construct meaning from a text.

8. A: Reading fluency is the ability to accurately read at a socially acceptable pace and with proper expression. Phonetic awareness leads to the proper pronunciation of words and fluency. Once students are able to read fluently, concentration is no longer dedicated toward the process of reading. Instead, students can concentrate on the meaning of a text. Thus, in the developmental process of reading, comprehension follows fluency.

Vocabulary, Academic Language, and Background Knowledge

1. B: When using contextual strategies, students are indirectly introduced to new words within a sentence or paragraph. Contextual strategies require students to infer the meaning(s) of new words. Word meaning is developed by utilizing semantic and contextual clues of the reading in which the word is located.

2. D: When reading, multiple strategies are used to decode and interpret the meaning of an unfamiliar word. Phonetics allows students to sound out the word. Structural analysis can be used to combine word parts in order to decode an unfamiliar term. Students can also use contextual clues within the sentence or paragraph that surround the unfamiliar term in order to derive its definition.

3. C: Word maps are visual organizers that promote structural analysis skills for vocabulary development. Word maps may be used to relate words that share a common morpheme. After being directly taught word morphology, students may be able to define an unfamiliar term by piecing together the meaning of the word's individual morphemes. In this way, word maps enable students to build upon background knowledge in order to gain comprehension of new words.

4. D: The problem in the original passage is that the second sentence is a dependent clause that cannot stand alone as a sentence; it must be attached to the main clause found in the first sentence. Because the main clause comes first, it does not need to be separated by a comma. However, if the dependent clause came first, then a comma would be necessary, which is why Choice *C* is incorrect. Choices *A* and *B* also insert unnecessary commas into the sentence.

5. A: The affix *circum–* originates from Latin and means "around or surrounding." It is also related to other words that indicate something round, such as circle and circus. The rest of the choices do not relate to the affix *circum–* and are therefore incorrect.

6. A: Only two of these suffixes, *–ize* and *–en*, can be used to form verbs, so Choices *B* and *D* are incorrect. Those choices create adjectives. The suffix *–ize* means "to convert or turn into." The suffix *–en* means "to become." Because this sentence is about converting ideas into money, money + –ize or *monetize* is the most appropriate word to complete the sentence, so Choice *C* is incorrect.

7. D: Students can use context clues to make a careful guess about the meaning of unfamiliar words. Although all of the words in a sentence can help contribute to the overall meaning, in this case, the adjective that pairs with *ubiquitous* gives the most important hint to the student: cars were first *rare*, but now they are *ubiquitous*. The inversion of *rare* is what gives meaning to the rest of the sentence; *ubiquitous* means "existing everywhere" or "not rare." Choice *A* is incorrect because *ago* only indicates a time frame. Choice *B* is incorrect because *cars* does not indicate a contrasting relationship to the word *ubiquitous* to provide a good context clue. Choice *C* is incorrect because it also only indicates a time frame, but used together with *rare*, it provides the contrasting relationship needed to identify the meaning of the unknown word.

8. C: A style guide offers advice about proper formatting, punctuation, and usage when writing for a specific field, such as journalism or scientific research. The other resources would not offer similar information. A dictionary is useful for looking up definitions; a thesaurus is useful for looking up synonyms and antonyms. A grammar book is useful for looking up specific grammar topics. Thus, Choices *A*, *B*, and *D* are incorrect.

9. B: A word's origin is also known as its *etymology*. In addition to offering a detailed list of a word's various meanings, a dictionary also provides information about a word's history, such as when it first came into use, what language it originated from, and how its meaning may have changed over time. A thesaurus is for identifying synonyms and antonyms, so Choice *A* is incorrect. A style guide provides formatting, punctuation, and syntactical advice for a specific field, and a grammar book is related to the appropriate placement of words and punctuation, which does not provide any insight into a word's origin. Therefore, Choices *C* and *D* are incorrect.

10. C: The .org domain on websites is generally used by nonprofit groups or community organizations. A government website uses .gov, and .edu is used for educational institutions. Private companies and businesses use .com, so Choices *A*, *B*, and *D* are incorrect.

11. D: Since the sentence contains two independent clauses and a dependent clause, the sentence is categorized as compound-complex:

Independent clause: *I accepted the change of seasons*

Independent clause: *I started to appreciate the fall*

Dependent clause: *Although I wished it were summer*

12. B: Since the sentence contains two independent clauses connected by a conjunction, it is referred to as a compound sentence.

Independent clause: *The teacher directed the children's attention to the diagram*

Independent clause: *The children couldn't understand the information*

Conjunction: *But*

13. D: The first sentence is written quite informally and gives a clear impression that the exchange is on a socially relaxed level. The second sentence is written quite formally and gives a clear impression that the exchange is academic or professional in nature. Although both sentences carry the same message—to respond to the messenger as quickly as possible—the register, or level of formality, is very different.

Accent refers to the way in which certain words are pronounced by an individual and is usually dependent on where a person resides. Dialect refers to how groups of people from a specific geographical region manipulate their language. Point of view refers to a person's interpretation of or feelings toward an event. In literature, a point of view refers to a character's interpretation of or feelings toward an event.

14. A: The three tiers of vocabulary are as follows:

> Conversational: informal, more relaxed

> Academic: more professional, with vocabulary intended to challenge critical thinking skills

> Domain-specific language: a unique vocabulary inventory that focuses on a given discipline or computer language

15. B: Word choice is the trait that teaches the use of precise language. Teachers can enhance this trait in students by helping them to use exact language that is accurate, concise, precise, and lively.

16. D: Intentional writing practice for the purpose of communicating refers to purposeful writing. Students can use this as a method of thinking through issues and solving problems related to writing.

17. C: Speaking, Listening, Reading, and Writing are the four elements of literacy development. As social beings, children begin to recognize that with effective literacy skills, their social, emotional, and physical needs can be met, and their curiosity can be satisfied.

18. C: Synonyms, Antonyms, and Homonyms are examples of semantic relationships. There are five types of semantic relationships, including the three noted in the question. The other two are Hyponyms and Meronyms.

19. B: A utilitarian combination of two or more languages that springs up where different linguistic groups overlap is known as a pidgin; it is used for communication tasks but not as a first language. However, when that pidgin becomes entrenched in the culture and is then taught to children as their first, native language, it is known as a Creole. *C* and *D* are not correct because they both refer to vocabulary, not to entire languages. Jargon is the vocabulary of a specific field or industry, and regionalisms are the vocabulary of a specific place.

Comprehension

1. D: Although the reading corner should be a restful and enjoyable place to encourage students to read independently, it does not enhance reading comprehension directly. Choices *A*, *B*, and *C* all encourage enhancement of reading comprehension. Giving students a chance to read independently allows them to choose books they enjoy, read at their own pace, and develop a lifelong enjoyment of reading.

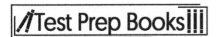

2. B: Purposeful teacher read-alouds allow students to listen to a story for voice emphasis and tone. This will help students when they are reading independently as well. Although students may find this time restful or a chance to catch up on old work, this is not the main purpose. Students may use this time to take notes on the reading, but students should only be listening to the story being read and not doing other work.

3. B: Pragmatics is the study of what words mean in certain situations. Choice *A*, morphology, involves the structure and formation of words. Choice *C*, syntax, refers to the order of words in a sentence. Choice *D*, semantics, addresses the distinct meanings of words.

4. A: "Text evidence" refers to taking phrases and sentences directly from the text and writing them in the answer. Students are not asked to paraphrase, nor use any other resources to address the answer. Therefore, Choices *B*, *C*, and *D* are incorrect.

5. C: The RICA for reading comprehension addresses the understanding of literal, inferential, and evaluative comprehension and various factors affecting reading comprehension. Nonfiction and fiction pieces are used on the RICA to address comprehension skills for the different text types such as reference documents, literature, and expository texts.

6. D: Text-based discussion, like think-pair-share, encourage all students to speak rather than having just one student share an answer. Each student is given time to collaborate with another student and share their thoughts. It is not intended for one student to give another student the answers, which is why Choice *C* is incorrect. Although Choices *A* and B might be correct, they are not the MOST important reason that group-based discussions are useful in the classroom.

7. D: Extension projects and papers should be used to challenge advanced learners, not learners developing comprehension skills. Graphic organizers, note taking, and small intervention groups can aid in reading comprehension. Graphic organizers and taking notes are great ways for a student to outline key parts of the text. Small intervention groups set up by the instructor can then focus on individual needs.

8. C: Advanced students can benefit from intervention groups by allowing the students to be challenged with more complex assignments. These assignments can be worked on independently and can include more difficult questions or higher-level vocabulary. Even short projects may be beneficial for these advanced students to work on throughout the week.

9. A: Small intervention groups can benefit from a teacher reading a text or small book aloud while students listen and take notes. This helps struggling students to not have to decode words but allows them to focus on reading comprehension. Intervention time is not meant for a teacher to give independent work nor to just provide observation without support.

10. B: Word analysis and fluency should be mastered before teaching theme, text evidence, and writing. For English Language Learners and struggling readers, word analysis and fluency are often difficult barriers, which is why comprehension skills are not initially mastered. Theme is often a complex and inferential skill, which is developed later on. Text evidence is pulling answers to comprehension questions directly from a text and cannot be accomplished until readers can fluently read and understand the text. Writing skills generally come after comprehension skills are underway.

11. C: Genre is a means of categorizing text by its structure and literary elements. Fiction and nonfiction are both genre categories. Plot is the sequence of events that makes a story happen.

12. A: Scanning future portions of the text for information that helps resolve a question is an example of self-monitoring. Self-monitoring takes advantage of the natural ability of students to recognize when they understand the reading and when they do not. KWL charts are used to help guide students to identify what they already know about a given topic. Metacognitive skills are when learners think about thinking. Directed reading-thinking activities are done before and after reading to improve critical thinking and reading comprehension.

13. C: Comprehension is the level of content understanding that a student demonstrates after reading. Orthographic development is a cumulative process for learning to read, with each skill building on the previously mastered skill. Fluency is an automatic recognition and accurate interpretation of text. Phonics is the ability to apply letter-sound relationships and letter patterns in order to accurately pronounce written words.

14. A: Voice is the primary trait that shows the individual writing style of an author. It is based on an author's choice of common syntax, diction, punctuation, character development, dialogue, etc.

15. B: The key word here is "inform," which is the primary purpose of all informative modes. They contain facts, definitions, instructions, and other elements with the objective purpose of informing a reader—such as study guides, instruction manuals, and textbooks. Choice *A* is incorrect because an argumentative mode contains language that is subjective and is intended to persuade or to inform with a persuasive bias. Choice *C* is incorrect as a narrative mode is used primarily to tell a story and has no intention of informing, nor is the language inherently objective. Choice *D* is incorrect as descriptive modes possess no inherent intent to inform and are used primarily to describe.

16. A: Editorials, recommendation letters, and cover letters all seek to persuade a reader to agree with the author, which reflects an argumentative mode. Choice *B* is incorrect because the intent of the examples is to persuade a reader to agree with the author, not to present information. Choice *C* is incorrect as editorials, letters of recommendation, and cover letters are not trying to tell a story. Choice *D* is also incorrect because while the examples may contain many descriptions, that is not their primary purpose.

Planning, Organizing, and Managing Reading Instruction Based on Ongoing Assessment

1. D: It is important for teachers to allocate time to work one-on-one with students who have IEPs. Students with IEPs may need to have skills retaught. Measuring the growth of students with IEPs can be done by charting their performance levels on a weekly basis. If there is little or no growth, a teacher may need to revisit their pacing or the form of instruction being used with the student(s).

2. A: Writing, language, speaking, and reading are all fundamental components needed for students to develop reading skills according to the California state reading standards. California state standards require the use of open-ended questions. Such assessments can be written or presented orally. Either way, students need to use textual evidence to support their responses. Therefore, good writing skills, language, and grammar development are essential.

3. D: The role of a reading specialist is not to tell teachers how to do their jobs, but rather to assist them. One role of a reading coach is to help teachers in their classrooms with assessing students or even teach lessons for teachers. Another role of a reading specialist is to inform staff of district changes at staff meetings, in-services, or in professional development opportunities. Such changes may include alterations of curriculum or state standards.

4. A: A reading corner is not designed to be a "hang out" for students. Rather, it is a place for students to share thoughts on books or discuss recommendations. A reading corner should have a fun atmosphere to enhance students' interest in reading and be filled with a variety of genres and levels.

5. B: Instruction should be differentiated. As students learn at different paces and levels, instruction should meet the needs of all students. This requires teachers to do ongoing assessments and group students according to these assessments. Grouping students may be based on needed skills or pacing of students.

6. C: In order to check assessments for validity, it's important to understand what both question types entail for students. Selected-response questions cover a broad range of topics in a shorter period of time. However, students can guess the correct response on selected-response questions. For example, a typical multiple-choice question provides four answers from which a student can choose. This gives students a 25 percent chance of guessing the correct answer. Therefore, the results of select-response assessments are not always valid. Open-ended questions are longer and more time-consuming. However, these questions assess students' skill levels more effectively. Open-ended assessments also allow students to use text-based evidence to support their answers.

7. D: Research is not a component of planning an effective reading lesson according to the California state standards. California state standards state that an effective reading lesson consists of presentations, direct instruction, guided practice, modeling, and intervention. Although a teacher may need to conduct research to provide a rich experience for their lesson, research is not a component of reading instruction according to the California state standards.

8. A: If the majority of the class did not master a skill taught, then the best plan is to reteach the skill to the entire class again. To break the class into intervention groups would not be the best use of time. Also, if too many students did not understand the skill, then perhaps the skill was not properly taught the first time. A different teaching approach may need to be used. The utilization of different types of media, more direct instruction, and modeling of the skill should be done several more times before the students are assessed on the skill a second time.

9. D: Good reading strategies are essential for all subject areas across the curriculum. In order to excel in science and social studies, there needs to be a good reading foundation—especially in nonfiction text. The United States documents or science and social studies textbooks may all be used to teach nonfiction. Informational magazines may have good nonfictional material, but these need to be selected carefully to ensure that the reading is appropriately substantive. Basal readers are also good examples of nonfiction text.

10. A: Intervention groups should be organized based on student performance. Although the behavior of students may be taken into consideration, the organization of group members should be primarily based on each student's performance levels.

128

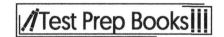

11. B: Students should carefully read what they've written during the evaluating stage of the POWER strategy.

12. B: Graphic organizers are used during the Organizing stage of the POWER strategy. They help students to examine, analyze, and summarize selections they have read and can be used individually or collaboratively in the classroom. Graphic organizers may be sequencing charts, graphs, Venn diagrams, timelines, chain of events organizers, story maps, concept maps, mind maps, webs, outlines, or other visual tools for connecting concepts to achieve understanding.

13. D: 6+1 Traits is a model for teaching writing that uses common language to explain writing standards. The 6+1 Traits are the characteristics that make writing readable and effective no matter what genre of writing is being used. These seven traits are ideas, organization, voice, word choice, sentence fluency, conventions, and presentation.

14. D: Organization is the trait that teaches students how to build the framework of their writing. Students choose an organizational strategy or purpose for the writing and build the details upon that structure. There are many purposes for writing, and they all have different frameworks.

15. C: Ideas ultimately form the content of the writing. The Ideas Trait is one of the 6+1 Traits model; it is where students learn to select an important topic for their writing. They are taught to narrow down and focus their idea before further developing it.

16. B: There are several effective assessments to evaluate a child's overall writing progress. Rating scales, student logs, and the POWER method are just some of these assessment methods. Although educators can create rating scales and student logs to assess and help students assess reading and spelling, the POWER method is specific to writing:

> P—Prewriting
>
> O—Organizing
>
> W—Writing a rough draft
>
> E—Evaluating
>
> R—Revise and Rewrite

17. D: In order for oral presentations to be effective, the presenter's volume should match the size of the audience and the location of the presentation. The presenter should also practice articulation—how clearly the words are being said. The third most important element of oral presentations is how well the presenter is engaging the audience. Making eye contact, moving around the room, and involving the audience, when appropriate, are all part of audience awareness skills.

18. A: Active listening skills are very important in all forms of communication, whether one is at home, among friends, in school, or at work. An active listener is one who pays close attention to what is being said, maintains eye contact, uses body language to indicate respect, asks relevant questions, and shares information that directly pertains to the subject.

19. D: Teachers use directed reading-thinking activities before and after reading to improve critical thinking and reading comprehension. Metacognitive skills are when learners think about their thinking.

129

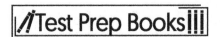

Self-monitoring is when children are asked to think as they read and ask themselves if what they have just read makes sense. KWL charts help guide students to identify what they already know about a given topic.

20. C: Asking oneself a comprehension question is a metacognition skill. Readers with metacognitive skills have learned to think about thinking. It gives students control over their learning while they read. KWL charts help students to identify what they already know about a given topic.

21. C: Listening and speaking are not part of Bloom's Taxonomy. The six parts are remembering, understanding, applying, analyzing, evaluating, and creating.

22. A: Reciprocal teaching involves predicting, summarizing, questioning, and clarifying. The other choices are all fictitious.

23. B: KWL charts are effective methods of activating prior knowledge and taking advantage of students' curiosity. Students can create a KWL (know/want to know/learned) chart to prepare for any unit of instruction and to generate questions about a topic.

24. C: The five basic components of reading education are phonemic awareness, phonics, fluency, vocabulary, and comprehension.

25. D: Cross-curricular integration is choosing to teach writing projects that include the subjects of science, social studies, mathematics, reading, etc.

Practice Test #2

Word Analysis

1. What is the most valuable strategy for helping children understand new words?
   a. Phonics instruction
   b. Pre-teaching
   c. Self-monitoring
   d. Context clues

2. A teacher wants to give students additional practice with visually similar letters, so he picks a story book that focuses on the letters *b* and *p*. The story includes repetition of pairs like *bat/pat, big/pig,* and *bin/pin*. After reading the story together, the teacher wants to select a supplementary activity to reinforce the skill. Which of the following would be the most useful activity?
   a. Have students practice writing the focus words from the story, but this time using capital letters.
   b. Put students into small groups to play a matching game, where each target word appears on two different cards and students have to recognize the words to make pairs.
   c. Have students brainstorm new words using the same rime but different onsets, such as *cat/sat/mat*.
   d. Ask for volunteers to retell the story from memory to the class.

3. Which of the following is NOT an example of a category of function words?
   a. Determiners
   b. Auxiliary verbs
   c. Pronouns
   d. Adverbs

4. A first-grade class is preparing an end-of-year talent show that will be attended by parents and other family members. At the end of the show, all of the students say, "Thank you, Mom and Dad!" However, during rehearsals, one English learner always says, "Tank you, Mom and Dad." Which of the following most likely accounts for his delivery of the word *thank*?
   a. His native language lacks the corresponding onset phoneme.
   b. He does not recognize the individual letters in the digraph.
   c. He needs more practice with consonant blends.
   d. He has not mastered the alphabetic principle.

5. Which of the following is an example of a word that ends with a continuous sound?
   a. Bought
   b. Created
   c. Passes
   d. Picnic

6. A second-grade teacher places students into small groups and gives each group a chart of a dozen different words, including *hippo, classroom, snowing,* and *bookshelf*. She then asks students to identify which words are compound words. What is she assessing through this activity?
    a. Students' ability to decode words based on their knowledge of morphemes
    b. Students' familiarity with grade-level vocabulary
    c. Students' ability to use prefixes and suffixes
    d. Students' knowledge of blending

7. A teacher conducts a miscue analysis by having a student read the following: "Schools around the globe have different types of recess for students. Some schools have structured time for supervised athletic activities, and other schools give students free time to chat with friends." When the student reads the sentences, she produces the following: "Schools around the world have different types of recess for students. Some schools have structured time for supervised athletic activities, and other schools give students free time to talk with friends." What type of word error would the teacher identify?
    a. Syntactic
    b. Visual
    c. Semantic
    d. Graphophonemic

8. Which of the following is an example of a pair of homophones?
    a. Look, book
    b. So, sew
    c. Lead, lead
    d. Kayak, radar

9. What are the two types of morphemes?
    a. Free and bound
    b. Prefixes and suffixes
    c. Greek and Latin
    d. Affixes and inflections

10. Which of the following words would be most suited to structural analysis?
    a. Familiarity
    b. Allowance
    c. Indestructible
    d. Sincere

11. Which of the following is an example of a word with an *r*-controlled vowel?
    a. Root
    b. Cart
    c. Trust
    d. Rain

12. How do *r*-controlled vowels differ from other vowels?
    a. They can only appear at the middle or end of a word.
    b. They are formed by single vowels, not diphthongs.
    c. They are neither long nor short.
    d. They always make the schwa sound.

13. Which of the following is an example of a CVC word?
    a. Pop
    b. See
    c. Are
    d. Oak

14. A teacher asks students to read the word *cup* and then replace /p/ with /t/ to form a new word. What activity is the teacher conducting?
    a. Sound deletion
    b. Sound substitution
    c. Sound segmentation
    d. Sound blending

15. A teacher shows the sentence, "The sky is blue," to students before reading it aloud and then asking them to identify how many words are in the sentence. What skill is the teacher assessing?
    a. Syllabication
    b. Morphological awareness
    c. Automaticity
    d. Word awareness

16. A student who has a strong grasp of monosyllabic words is struggling to understand multisyllabic words. How can the teacher help the student develop her syllable awareness skills?
    a. Have the student incorporate physical motion when she reads multisyllabic words, such as clapping or tapping the desk to count syllables.
    b. Have the student write a list of target words and then draw lines for her to indicate syllable breaks in each word.
    c. Show her how to use the dictionary to locate a word's pronunciation and syllable divisions.
    d. Explain that each syllable has a single vowel sound.

17. What is schwa?
    a. The most common vowel sound in spoken English, such as the first vowel in *banana*
    b. The vowel sound produced by two adjacent vowels, such as in the word *bear*
    c. The silent letters that appear in words such as *listen* and *lamb*
    d. The function of consonants as vowels, such as in *sky* and *cow*

18. A teacher shares the following set of words with her students: *cap, pat, sad*. She then asks students what sound they have in common. What skill is she assessing?
    a. Alphabetic principle
    b. Phonetic spelling
    c. Sound identity
    d. Digraph blending

133

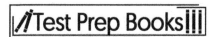
19. Which of the following is an example of a graphophonemic miscue?
    a. A student misreads *faith* as *father*.
    b. A student misreads *improper* as *unproper*.
    c. A student misreads *taken* as *take*.
    d. A student misreads *large* as *big*.

20. What is true of the relationship between graphemes and phonemes?
    a. Each phoneme corresponds to a single grapheme.
    b. Graphemes are combinations of letters that, in turn, produce phonemes.
    c. Graphemes are the letter(s) that represent phonemes.
    d. Phonemes are related to pronunciation, whereas graphemes are not.

21. In a first-grade class, a teacher brings a collection of pictures cut out from newspapers and magazines. Students are instructed to choose a couple of pictures, write sentences or a short story about the pictures, and then share what they've written. One student is reluctant to share his writing, though, because he is worried about his spelling—for example, he has a hard time remembering how to spell *would* and writes *wud* instead. What would be an appropriate response from the teacher?
    a. Assure him that it's fine to try his best to spell a word how he thinks it sounds.
    b. Give him additional practice in phonemic awareness.
    c. Correct all of his spelling on in-class assignments.
    d. Allow him to deliver his story orally rather than in writing.

22. How should teachers approach common words with irregular or uncommon spellings, such as *said* and *goes*?
    a. Let students learn them implicitly through repeated exposure in text.
    b. Teach them as sight words through direct instruction.
    c. Explain the etymology that leads to diverse spelling patterns in English.
    d. Ignore them in favor of high-frequency words with regular spelling patterns.

23. Which of the following is an example of a word that ends with an open syllable?
    a. Speeches
    b. Education
    c. Beginning
    d. Birthday

24. Which of the following is an example of a word family used in building phonemic awareness in readers?
    a. Eat, ate, eaten
    b. Bat, mat, sat
    c. Dog, cat, mouse
    d. Wind, unwind, rewind

25. What best characterizes a student who has mastered letter recognition?
    a. A student is able to recite the alphabet in order.
    b. A student is able to produce both print and cursive letters.
    c. A student is able to recognize upper- and lowercase letters as well as the sounds and names of letters.
    d. A student is able to recognize that a letter is the same even when it produces different sounds in different words.

26. A class is starting to learn consonant digraphs. Which would be the most appropriate ending digraph sound to learn for a beginning reading class?
    a. /sh/ in bush
    b. /gh/ in though
    c. /ey/ in they
    d. /ou/ in you

27. A fourth-grade class is going to take a field trip to an American history museum. Before the trip, students read an informative article about the founding of America and the Revolutionary War. One student volunteers to read aloud to the class, and she reads the words "Constitution" and "Declaration of Independence" with the correct stress and pronunciation. However, after she has finished reading, the teacher asks if she has heard of those documents before, and she says no. Which of the following best explains how she arrived at her correct pronunciation of those words?
    a. Even if she doesn't know exactly what they mean, she has probably encountered them in print before and was able to make a close guess as to their meaning and pronunciation.
    b. She knew how to pronounce the base words, *constitute* and *declare,* and applied that knowledge to pronouncing their derived forms.
    c. The class has read several other history-related texts before, so she already had practice pronouncing academic vocabulary from that subject.
    d. She recognized the orthographic pattern *-tion* and understood that words with that ending place stress on the penultimate syllable.

Constructed Response

Instructions: Prepare an organized written response to the following topic. Your response should be 150 to 300 words.

Scenario: One elementary school teacher has been demonstrating word analysis strategies over the course of the last week. He has emphasized how word analysis illuminates the meanings of both words and texts. Now, his students are ready to utilize these strategies independently as they begin reading a new book.

Task 1: Describe some strategies that the teacher might have presented to his students and how such strategies could help students decipher unknown words as they read the new book.

Task 2: Explain how students' awareness of context and theme creates a better understanding of phonetic meaning, and, alternatively, how students' knowledge of phonetic meaning informs their understanding of context and theme.

135

Fluency

1. What area of study involves mechanics, usage, and sentence formation?
   a. Word analysis
   b. Spelling conventions
   c. Morphemes
   d. Phonics

2. Reading fluency involves what key areas?
   a. Accuracy, rate, and prosody
   b. Accuracy, rate, and consistency
   c. Prosody, accuracy, and clarity
   d. Rate, prosody, and comprehension

3. A child reads the story "Little Red Riding Hood" aloud. He easily pronounces the words, uses an apprehensive tone to show that the main character should not be leaving the path, adds a scary voice for the Big Bad Wolf, and reads the story at a pace that engages the class. What are these promising signs of?
   a. Reading fluency
   b. Phonemic awareness
   c. Reading comprehension
   d. Working memory

4. Poetry is often an effective device when teaching what skill?
   a. Fluency
   b. Spelling
   c. Writing
   d. Word decoding

5. Reading fluency is best described as the ability to do what?
   a. Read smoothly and accurately
   b. Comprehend what is read
   c. Demonstrate phonetic awareness
   d. Properly pronounce a list of words

6. A teacher is in the midst of creating a unit in which he hopes to further promote students' reading skills. In this process, the teacher should make sure that:
   a. Vocabulary development is central to all activities within the unit.
   b. Data from student reading assessments is used to target reading skills that reflect the students' needs.
   c. Students are required to use words provided on a word wall within multiple writing assignments.
   d. Instruction is the same for all students.

7. A teacher needs to assess students' accuracy in reading high frequency sight words and irregular sight words that are grade-appropriate. Which of the following strategies would be most appropriate for this purpose?
   a. The teacher gives students a list of words to study for a spelling test that will be administered the following week.
   b. The teacher allows students to bring their favorite books from home and has them read their selected text aloud independently.
   c. The teacher administers the Stanford structural analysis assessment to determine students' rote memory and application of morphemes contained within the words.
   d. The teacher records how many words each student reads correctly when reading aloud a list of teacher-selected, grade-appropriate words.

8. Which of the following is true of first language acquisition?
   a. Children need some instruction from parents or caregivers to learn a first language.
   b. Children first begin forming complete words when they are about two years old.
   c. Children experiment with the sounds of a language before they form words.
   d. Children have no language comprehension before they can speak.

Constructed Response

Instructions: Prepare an organized written response to the following topic. Your response should be 75 to 125 words.

Scenario: At the beginning of the school year, a teacher is presented with a class of students who vary widely in terms of fluency. On an initial fluency assessment, a few students scored very low, other students score very high, and most scored somewhere in between. The teacher knows that she must make reading practice neither too easy nor too difficult for any of her students.

Task 1: Identify and briefly discuss several strategies a classroom teacher could use to increase student fluency, specifically in a classroom of students whose base level of fluency varies widely.

Task 2: Explain how these strategies will increase student fluency and how a teacher should set different milestones for students at varying reading levels.

Vocabulary, Academic Language, and Background Knowledge

1. Which of the following is true of Standard English?
   a. It is one dialect of English.
   b. It is the original form of English.
   c. It is the most complex form of English.
   d. It is the form that follows grammatical rules.

2. A teacher notices that when students are talking to each other between classes, they are using their own unique vocabulary words and expressions to talk about their daily lives. When the teacher hears these non-standard words that are specific to one age or cultural group, what type of language is she listening to?
   a. Slang
   b. Jargon
   c. Dialect
   d. Vernacular

3. A teacher wants to counsel a student about using the word *ain't* in a research paper for a high school English class. What advice should the teacher give?
   a. *Ain't* is not in the dictionary, so it isn't a word.
   b. Because the student isn't in college yet, *ain't* is an appropriate expression for a high school writer.
   c. *Ain't* is incorrect English and should not be part of a serious student's vocabulary because it sounds uneducated.
   d. *Ain't* is a colloquial expression, and while it may be appropriate in a conversational setting, it is not standard in academic writing.

4. A ninth-grade class is reading a novel together. After each chapter, they have a class discussion where students take turns summarizing the plot, sharing observations and reactions, and answering questions posed by the teacher. One question the teacher asks is, "How would you describe the diction in the text?" What is the teacher referring to?
   a. The unknown words students encounter in the text and want to learn
   b. The author's use of specific language in foreshadowing
   c. The words students recognize from earlier vocabulary instruction
   d. The author's word choice that contributes to the style and mood

5. A teacher asks his students to keep a class notebook during the semester. The notebook includes a section where they self-evaluate their study habits and identify areas they can improve. What is the main skill the teacher is targeting through this activity?
   a. Organization
   b. Daily writing habits
   c. Metacognition
   d. Test preparation

6. What are the three key factors to consider when selecting appropriate vocabulary terms for a class?
   a. Frequency, utility, and students' level of knowledge
   b. Etymology, spelling difficulty, and academic usage
   c. Word families, affixes, and common roots
   d. Literary, academic, and everyday

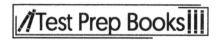

7. In vocabulary instruction for English Language Learners, what is a disadvantage of relying on cognates?
   a. Students can get confused with false cognates, hindering comprehension.
   b. Students will lose motivation to study English because they will find it too easy.
   c. Not every language has the same number of cognates in English, so it creates an unfair advantage for students who speak closely related languages.
   d. Most cognates are related to conversational words, not academic vocabulary.

8. A fourth-grade class is reading a short story about a girl who starts a Victory Garden during World War II. The teacher decides to include an accompanying informational text about rationing and other home-front efforts during the war. When selecting an appropriate reading level for the informational text, the teacher should select something that does which of the following?
   a. Matches students' frustration reading level.
   b. Matches students' independent reading level.
   c. Matches students' instructional reading level.
   d. Matches students' comprehension reading level.

9. A seventh-grade teacher introduces a week-long unit on rain forest conservation, and she begins the lesson by having students start a KWL chart on the board. Why did she include this activity?
   a. She wants to motivate students by having them engage in a competitive game.
   b. She wants to activate students' background knowledge on the subject.
   c. She wants to figure out which students are most interested in the topic.
   d. She wants to have students practice formal writing responses.

10. A student is struggling with multiple-choice questions related to academic reading passages. When his teacher asks him to summarize the contents of the passage, he is able to identify and explain the main ideas. Also, his short-answer responses are generally high scoring. How can his teacher help him improve his overall test scores?
    a. Give him additional vocabulary homework focused on high-frequency academic words.
    b. Give him additional time to complete practice tests.
    c. Give him additional background reading about grade-level-appropriate academic topics.
    d. Give him additional practice in identifying and responding to different question types.

11. A teacher prepared a list of need-to-know academic vocabulary words for students to master by the end of the semester, including words such as *analyze, observation,* and *hypothesize.* Which tier of vocabulary best describes these words?
    a. Tier 1
    b. Tier 2
    c. Tier 3
    d. Tier 4

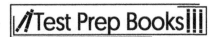

12. In academic reading contexts, what is an advantage of building students' sight word vocabulary?
   a. The future academic texts that students will encounter during their education will primarily consist of sight words.
   b. Students will not have to stop and decode every word and can instead improve their reading rate and focus on overall textual comprehension.
   c. Most sight words form the roots of academic vocabulary, so students will be able to infer the meanings of unfamiliar words.
   d. Sight words contain all forty-four phonemes found in English, which can aid with academic vocabulary pronunciation.

13. A teacher wants students to learn academic vocabulary related to the root *cred*. Which of the following is an example of vocabulary instruction through reciprocal teaching?
   a. Students identify instances of words using *cred* in their daily reading and homework assignments during the week and write the words in a personal vocabulary log.
   b. Students are given a list of relevant words, such as *credible, discredit*, and *credulity*, and the teacher explains the meanings and usage of each.
   c. Students are given a list of relevant words and must write ten practice sentences using the words in context.
   d. Students are given several examples of *cred* before brainstorming other examples together and are then put in pairs and assigned one new *cred* word to introduce to the class.

14. Which of the following is an example of a pair of synonyms?
   a. Click, trick
   b. Happy, joyful
   c. Excited, disappointed
   d. Philosophy, sophisticated

15. A teacher wants to introduce a Word of the Day as part of classroom language enrichment. Which of the following is the most useful way to incorporate the project into class?
   a. She should not start a Word of the Day because research shows that students have low retention of daily vocabulary and are not able to fully learn more than three new vocabulary words per week.
   b. She should make a poster on the wall with the Word of the Day, add one word to it every day, and then take it down and change it at the end of the week.
   c. She should introduce the word through explicit instruction and then give students a chance to read and write the word in context.
   d. She should give students a weekly quiz in which they have to match words and definitions.

16. Students are assigned to read the following passage: "In the king's court, flattery was the surest path to success. The most powerful courtier was also the most obsequious." The teacher asks his students to use context clues to come up with a general definition for *obsequious*. Which of the following best describes how to use context clues in this situation?
   a. The students should refer to a glossary or a footnote in the text that provides explanations for specific terms.
   b. The students should consider the part of speech and the words closely surrounding the unknown term.
   c. The students should get in small groups to share their ideas about the definition of the term.
   d. The students should recall their previous knowledge of historical texts.

140

17. Which of the following is the most helpful for guiding classroom dictionary usages?
- a. Students should have limited access to dictionaries because they should be able to decode most new vocabulary using other skills, such as word analysis and context clues.
- b. ELs should be able to access dictionaries during in-class writing, but they are generally not necessary for native English speakers.
- c. Students should learn that the first dictionary definition is always the most commonly used one.
- d. Students should learn to recognize the different information contained within a dictionary entry, such as spelling, pronunciation, multiple definitions, and word origins.

18. A teacher gives students a list of vocabulary words pulled from a poetry unit and asks them to identify how comfortable they are using each word. Which category would be appropriate to describe words that a student has encountered before but is not fully confident using yet?
- a. Unknown words
- b. Acquainted words
- c. Auditory words
- d. Established words

19. Which of the following is true of about instruction in an English classroom?
- a. In English class, instruction should emphasize reading and writing.
- b. Teachers should place students in small groups with other students with similar learning styles and allow for differentiated instruction that focuses on their language strengths.
- c. Kinesthetic and tactile lessons are important for early learners, while older students can focus almost exclusively on written texts.
- d. Students should be immersed in a language-rich environment where they can explore new words through reading, writing, listening, and speaking.

Constructed Response

Instructions: Prepare an organized written response to the following topic. Your response should be 75 to 125 words.

Scenario: After working with several groups of students throughout the school, a reading coach notices that her students are struggling to comprehend reading material about specific content areas. She talks with classroom teachers about her observations, and they decide to merge reading instruction with content area instruction to boost comprehension.

Task 1: Briefly describe how a reaching coach can organize exercises to emphasize content-specific information.

Task 2: Discuss how combined content area instruction and reading instruction may impact reading comprehension.

Comprehension

1. The type of writing mode an author chooses to use is dependent on which of the following elements?

> I. The audience
> > II. The primary purpose
> > III. The main idea

a. III only
b. I and II
c. I and III
d. I, II, and III

2. Which of the following refers to what an author wants to express about a given subject?
    a. Primary purpose
    b. Plot
    c. Main idea
    d. Characterization

3. Which organizational style is used in the following passage?
    There are several reasons why the new student café has not been as successful as expected.
    One factor is that prices are higher than originally advertised, so many students cannot afford to
    buy food and beverages there. Also, the café closes rather early; as a result, students go out into
    town to other late-night gathering places rather than meeting friends at the café on campus.

    a. Cause and effect order
    b. Compare and contrast order
    c. Spatial order
    d. Time order

4. Short, succinct sentences are best written for which of the following audiences?
    a. Adults or people more familiar with a subject
    b. Children or people less familiar with a subject
    c. Politicians and academics
    d. University students

5. Which of the following defines the stage of writing that involves adding to, removing, rearranging, or
re-writing sections of a piece?
    a. The revising stage
    b. The publishing stage
    c. The writing stage
    d. The pre-writing stage

6. When students study character development, setting, and plot, what are they most likely studying?
    a. Word analysis
    b. Point of view
    c. Literary analysis of a fictional text
    d. Fluency

7. The author's purpose, major ideas, supporting details, visual aids, and vocabulary are the five key
elements of what type of text?
    a. Fictional texts
    b. Narratives
    c. Persuasive texts
    d. Informational texts

8. When students use inference, what are they able to do?
    a. Make logical assumptions based on contextual clues.
    b. Independently navigate various types of text.
    c. Summarize a text's main idea.
    d. Paraphrase a text's main idea.

9. Story maps, an effective instructional tool, help children to do all of the following EXCEPT:
    a. Analyze relationships among characters, events, and ideas in literature.
    b. Understand key details of a story.
    c. Follow the story's development.
    d. Read at a faster pace.

10. Which text feature does NOT help a reader locate information in printed or digital text?
    a. Hyperlink
    b. Sidebar
    c. Glossary
    d. Heading

11. Read the following sentences to answer the question below:
    He is a kind and generous man who wants nothing more than the best for his community,
    thought Michael as the board members discussed the nominees for head of council. Lana June,
    however, was far more critical. *He is just saying those things to get elected,* she thought.

What is the author's point of view?
    a. First person
    b. Third person limited
    c. Third person omniscient
    d. Objective

12. Autobiographies and memoirs are examples of what form of writing?
    a. Fiction
    b. Narrative
    c. Informational text
    d. Research papers

13. Which effective writing area engages and connects with the audience, igniting emotion?
    a. Ethos
    b. Logos
    c. Pathos
    d. Kairos

14. First-hand accounts of an event, subject matter, time period, or person are referred to as what type of source?
    a. Primary sources
    b. Secondary sources
    c. Direct sources
    d. Indirect sources

143

15. What type of literary device is being used in this sentence?
I worked a billion hours this week!

   a. Idiom
   b. Metaphor
   c. Hyperbole
   d. Alliteration

16. What technique might an author use to let the reader know that the main character was in a car crash as a child?
   a. Point of view
   b. Characterization
   c. Figurative language
   d. Flashback

Constructed Response

Instructions: Prepare an organized written response to the following topic. Your response should be 150 to 300 words.

Scenario: Several weeks into the school year, a teacher notices that many of her students have been struggling with the reading material she has assigned. Some of these students struggle with reading comprehension in general, while other students struggle with reading comprehension related to specific subjects. Her students have difficulty identifying connections between texts and making inferences.

Task 1: Describe how a teacher can organize class instruction to facilitate increased student engagement with reading material and identify exercises she can use to encourage her students both to draw inferences about a text and to make connections between texts.

Task 2: Briefly explain the relationship between vocabulary and comprehension, as well as between academic language and comprehension.

Planning, Organizing, and Managing Reading Instruction Based on Ongoing Assessment

1. If diagnostic assessments indicate students have phonetic problems, which of the following activities would be best for the instructor to introduce?
   a. Activities that analyze the different aspects of words.
   b. Activities that help students visualize what they read.
   c. Activities that have students paraphrase and summarize texts.
   d. Activities that involve using graphic organizers to identify key points and supporting details in texts.

2. A student takes a standardized formal reading assessment and achieves a score that lands them in the 77th percentile. What does this mean?
   a. The student answered 77 percent of the questions correctly.
   b. The student answered 77 questions correctly.
   c. The student performed better than 77 percent of test takers.

d. 77 percent of test takers scored higher than the student.

3. Which of the following is an example of interest-based differentiation?
   a. Grouping students who are all struggling with comprehending grade-level vocabulary words.
   b. Grouping students who are all working on reading fluency.
   c. Grouping students who are all working on sounding out unfamiliar words when reading aloud.
   d. Grouping students who are all auditory learners.

4. Which of the following best describes differentiated reading instruction?
   a. Students follow their own unique curriculum focused on individual strengths and needs.
   b. Reading exercises are geared toward students' literary preferences and sensibilities.
   c. Classrooms are geared toward whole-class instruction.
   d. Students work at their own reading level to achieve learning goals.

5. A student's ability to do which of the following indicates a high level of engagement with a text?
   a. Make inferences and analyze large bits of text
   b. Concisely summarize large bits of text
   c. Construct grammatically correct sentences that are free of spelling errors
   d. Recall specific facts and details from the text

6. In class discussions, small group activities, and written exercises, which is the best way to engage students at different reading levels?
   a. Focus on a single text
   b. Focus on a larger context, topic, or theme
   c. Focus on each students' distinct impressions of a text
   d. Have all students read the same selection of texts

7. The activation of prior knowledge, construction of prerequisite knowledge, commitment to intentional practice, and intermittent introduction of more complex reading material are examples of which strategy?
   a. Modeling
   b. Scaffolding
   c. Individualized instruction
   d. Differentiated instruction

8. What role does modeling play in effective instructional delivery?
   a. Teachers demonstrate how students should think about a text.
   b. Teachers provide a positive learning environment where students can think freely.
   c. Teachers demonstrate good reading behaviors and verbalize comprehension processes.
   d. Teachers highlight the parts of a text that students should know and memorize.

9. Which best describes the role of reading coaches?
   a. They develop a curriculum for struggling readers that classroom teachers follow.
   b. They work with struggling readers exclusively after school to develop better reading strategies.
   c. They coordinate their curricula with those of the classroom teachers to reinforce reading strategies.
   d. They act as a liaison between classroom teachers and parents/caretakers.

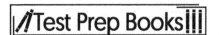
10. Why might teachers use student self-assessments in their reading curricula?
    a. To accumulate accurate assessment data
    b. To communicate students' needs to their parents and caretakers
    c. To develop individualized learning goals
    d. To reduce student distractions

11. Which best describes how reading material and instruction should be organized to target a student's zone of proximal development?
    a. They should be geared toward skills not yet acquired.
    b. They should reinforce existing skills while building new skills.
    c. They should focus on correcting mistakes made in previous units.
    d. They should be consistent for a whole class.

12. Which best describes how teachers should use assessment data about students' reading levels?
    a. To identify which supports are required for a student to work with more complex material
    b. To develop an individualized reading curriculum focused on a student's current reading level
    c. To design class work, assignments, and tests based on the average reading level of the class
    d. To provide detailed class reports and statistics for school administrators and parents

13. What is scaffolding?
    a. A support network that includes reading coaches and caretakers
    b. Temporary supports that help students access more complex texts
    c. Effective reading strategies taught to all students in a class
    d. A collection of physical locations, such as reading rooms and libraries, where students receive reading support

14. In a classroom, students are broken into three small groups. One group responds to a reading by making a mural, a second group writes a paragraph response, and a third group performs a skit. What method of instruction did the teacher employ?
    a. Individualized instruction
    b. Differentiated instruction
    c. Direct instruction
    d. Whole-class instruction

15. At what point should teachers offer reading interventions to struggling students?
    a. When it becomes apparent that a student is falling behind
    b. After a student proves incapable of independently working through difficult material
    c. When a student's support network requests such strategies
    d. Whenever a student makes more than one mistake per reading session

16. Which of the following is NOT a principle of classroom reading instruction?
    a. Teachers provide clear feedback when students make mistakes.
    b. Teachers provide students many opportunities to respond to questions.
    c. Teachers give students time to read aloud with a peer or in small groups.
    d. Teachers use whole-group instruction to accelerate student learning.

17. Which type of reading assessment identifies deficiencies in specific reading skill areas, like phonics?
    a. Outcomes assessment
    b. Screening assessment
    c. Progress monitoring assessment
    d. Diagnostic assessment

18. Which best describes a fluency assessment?
    a. Students read aloud for a minute, and teachers track how many words are pronounced correctly and how many words are pronounced incorrectly or skipped.
    b. Students read aloud selected words from a worksheet or words that the teacher singles out in a text, and the teacher record mistakes.
    c. Students are prompted to break words into parts and sound them out by putting phonetic parts together.
    d. Students read a complete text and answer questions that ask them to identify factual details and draw inferences about the text.

19. Which of the following helps create a literacy-rich environment?
    a. Newsletters about student reading goals that are sent to parents once a month
    b. Encouraging classroom discussion on free choice reading books
    c. Weekly evaluation meetings between grade-level reading teachers and reading coaches
    d. Displaying student work on classroom walls

20. Which of the following describes a meaning-based mistake on an oral assessment?
    a. Substituting one word in a passage for another word that makes sense in context
    b. Substituting equivalent parts of speech, like those for some
    c. Substituting one word in a passage for another word that looks similar, like boot for boom
    d. Substituting similar sounding words without registering differences in meaning

21. How do reading assessments aid instruction?
    a. Reading assessments provide fair metrics for assigning grades.
    b. Reading assessments reveal students' strengths and weaknesses and help teachers plan instruction.
    c. Reading assessments show teachers who needs an IEP.
    d. Reading coaches use results from reading assessments to help students outside the classroom.

22. A student who makes more than one error per ten words while reading is performing at what reading level?
    a. Instructional
    b. Independent
    c. Frustration
    d. Emergent

23. Why should a student practice reading at his or her instructional reading level?
    a. Students build confidence by practicing with familiar reading material.
    b. Students only develop reading skills by encountering challenging words.
    c. Students need to practice at the same reading level for several months at a time.
    d. Students benefit from working with both new and familiar words.

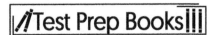

24. Which of the following should teachers NOT do when communicating assessment results to parents?
    a. Familiarize parents with the structure and presentation of test questions
    b. Provide resources and methods for helping their child practice reading skills
    c. Point out the areas in which their child struggles
    d. Focus on assessment scores in isolation, not in conjunction with classwork to that point

25. Typically, how frequently do reading teachers administer progress monitoring assessments?
    a. Once a month
    b. At the beginning and end of every school year
    c. Once a week or every other week
    d. At the beginning and end of every unit

Constructed Response: Case Study

Instructions: Prepare an organized written response to a case study of an elementary student. Your response should be 300 to 600 words and address information pertinent to each of the five domains.

Scenario: The following case study is based on three third grade students in Ms. Jones's class: Logan, Sasha, and Tyrone. Logan scored very high on all of his reading assessments throughout the first semester, and Ms. Jones placed him in a small group with other students who also received high marks on their reading assessments. Sasha, on the other hand, scored quite low on her first semester reading assessments. Ms. Jones expected that Sasha would struggle with these assessments because Sasha's second-grade teacher flagged her as at-risk to fall behind her classmates. Additionally, Sasha scored poorly on the screening assessment that Ms. Jones gave her in the first week of class. Ms. Jones placed Sasha in a small group with other students who struggle with reading.

Finally, Tyrone scored somewhere between Logan's scores and Sasha's scores, so Ms. Jones placed him in a small group with other students who scored at a similar reading level. Every student in Ms. Jones's class, regardless of reading level, read the same book, but their final assignments varied depending on their small group placement. Logan's group was required to write and perform a play about themes from the book. His group cooperated well with one another. Meanwhile, Tyrone's group worked mostly independently of one another. Each student in Tyrone's group was expected to complete a written response to the book, and their responses were expected to cover big picture elements of the book, like its historical context. Finally, Sasha's group was required to complete a poster that depicted the historical context, setting, and tone of the book. To Ms. Jones's surprise, none of the small groups managed to produce responses that spoke to the big picture elements of the book. Worse still, each small group seemed confused about the meaning of the story.

Using the information in the scenario and the notes below, respond to each of the tasks in a way that displays your understanding of literacy assessment and instructional strategies.

Teacher Notes:

- While Logan's group produced a skit that included some quoted material from the text, his group struggled to understand how those factual details fit together in a larger context.

- The students from Tyrone's group identified the characters in the story, but they were unable to explain the causal links between character actions or make inferences about their behaviors.

148

- Ms. Jones was pleased to see that Sasha's group produced a poster that accurately depicted the physical characteristics of the story's major characters, but their poster was devoid of contextual details.

- Each group was expected to complete a word bank as part of their final assignment. While most groups provided denotatively accurate definitions of new and significant words, many definitions were connotatively irrelevant.

Your response should completely address the following tasks:

Task 1: Based on the descriptions of each student, assess how well Ms. Jones organized class instruction based on the reading assessment results. Could she have used reading assessments differently? How else could she have integrated reading assessments with planning and organization?

Task 2: Identify the methods Ms. Jones could use to boost reading comprehension. Describe how vocabulary, academic language, and background knowledge impact comprehension, and evaluate how well Ms. Jones deployed classroom instruction to target vocabulary, academic language, and background knowledge. Describe word analysis and fluency exercises that Ms. Jones could assign to small groups and how those exercises would adapt to each of the three groups depicted in the case study.

Note: the 6 domains are as follows.

1. Word Analysis

2. Fluency

3. Vocabulary, Academic Language, and Background Knowledge

4. Comprehension

5. Planning, Organizing, and Managing Reading Instruction Based on Ongoing Assessment

Answer Explanations #2

Word Analysis

1. B: Pre-teaching is the most valuable strategy for helping children understand new words. Educators select what they evaluate to be the unfamiliar words in the text and then introduce them to the class before reading. Educators using this method should be careful not to simply ask the children to read the text and then spell the new words correctly.

2. B: Put students into small groups to play a matching game where each target word appears on two different cards and students have to recognize the words to make pairs. In this situation, the teacher wants students to focus on the difference between the similar letter shapes *b* and *p*. The matching game requires students to pay attention to the form of the letters and also allows students to practice recognizing and reading the same words they have just heard in the story. Choice *A* is not the best answer because the capital letters *B* and *P* do not require the same type of differentiation as their lowercase forms. Choice *C* is appropriate for allowing students to connect new words with ones they already know but does not reinforce the target lesson. Choice *D* is also a way to assess comprehension, but again, does not target the specific *b* and *p* skill.

3. D: Adverbs are not a category of function words. Function words are contrasted with content words. While content words convey the unique meanings of the sentence, function words serve largely grammatical roles to help structure the sentence. For example, words such as *destroy, daily,* and *warm* are content words, while words such as *the, to,* and *can* are function words. Function words include words such as determiners, Choice *A*, auxiliary verbs, Choice *B*, pronouns, Choice *C*, and prepositions.

4. A: His native language lacks the corresponding onset phoneme. The phoneme /th/ does not appear in many languages, so English Language Learners may replace it with /s/ or /t/. Students may be able to recognize the phoneme even if they cannot produce it, so Choices *B* is not the best answer. Choice *C* is incorrect because /th/ is an example of a digraph, not a consonant blend.

5. C: *Passes* ends in a continuous sound. A continuous sound is one that can be held and extended, in contrast to stop sounds. Whether a word ends with a continuous or stop sounds affects its pronunciation. Examples of continuous sounds are /s/, /r/, and /z/, while examples of stop sounds are /t/, /d/, and /k/.

6. A: Students' ability to decode words based on their knowledge of morphemes. Morphemes are the smallest units of individual meaning in a language; compound words such as *classroom* and *bookshelf* consist of two morphemes that combine to form a new word. Compound words allow students to apply their existing vocabulary to discover new words. Choice *C* is incorrect because prefixes and suffixes include examples such as *un-, pre-, -tion,* and *-ible,* which are all useful morphemes for decoding language but are not the same as compound words. Choice *D* is incorrect because blending involves combining letter sounds, not words.

7. C: This is an example of a semantic error, which is sometimes referred to as an error in meaning. In the example, the student replaced *globe* with *world* and *chat* with *talk*. The substitutions fit the context of the sentence and are not incorrect in meaning; in this type of error, the student anticipates the meaning of the sentence and uses the word they expect to see, regardless of whether it actually appears in the sentence. A syntactic miscue, Choice *A*, is one that preserves the grammar of the sentence (for example, reading *the* instead of *a*), while a graphophonemic miscue, Choice *D*, occurs when a student mispronounces a word or replaces it with something that looks similar (for example, *tough* instead of *though*).

8. B: *So* and *sew* are homophones. Homophone literally means "same sound"; homophones are words that are spelled differently but pronounced the same.

9. A: The two types of morphemes are free and bound. Free morphemes are those that can stand alone as words with independent meaning (sometimes referred to as base or root words), while bound morphemes are affixes (prefixes, suffixes, inflectional affixes) that must be attached to a free morpheme to have meaning. For example, in the word *unknown, known* is a free morpheme, and *un-* is a bound morpheme.

10. C: Structural analysis asks students to break a word down into its component parts of free and bound morphemes to decode its meaning. As such, words that contain a root with many affixes are most useful for this approach. *Indestructible* has two affixes, *in-* and *-ble,* attached to the root *destruct,* so it is well suited to this type of analysis.

11. B: *R*-controlled vowels are those that are followed by the letter *r*, transforming the sound (compare the vowel sounds in *cart* and *cat*). Thus, the correct answer is *cart.*

12. C: They are neither long nor short. As in the previous example, compare the sound produced by a short vowel such as in *cat* with the *r*-controlled vowel in *cart,* or the long vowel produced by *care* with the *r*-controlled vowel in *car.*

13. A: *Pop* is a CVC word. CVC refers to the word's spelling—consonant, vowel, consonant. Other common patterns in English include VC, CVCC, and CVVC words, among others.

14. B: The ability to replace one sound with another, often to produce a new word, is called sound substitution.

15. D: The teacher is assessing students' ability to recognize individual words as discrete units of meaning, which is considered word analysis.

16. A: Have the student incorporate physical motion when she reads multisyllabic words, such as clapping or tapping the desk to count syllables. Incorporating physical motion is a useful strategy to help the student become more aware of the individual sounds as she produces them. Choice *B* is not the best answer because it only helps her read the target words but doesn't provide a skill she can use independently. Choice *C* is also not the best answer for an early learner and would be time consuming for decoding everyday text. Choice *D* is also not the best way to provide a practical skill.

17. A: *Schwa* is the most common vowel sound in spoken English, such as the first vowel in *banana*. Although *schwa* does not appear in written English, it is the most commonly produced sound in spoken

English. It sounds something like *uh* and is generally heard in unstressed syllables, such as the first and last syllables in the word *banana;* only the middle, stressed syllable produces a clear *a* sound.

18. C: Sound identity refers to the ability to recognize and identify sounds in context.

19. A: Graphophonemic errors are those in which the student misreads the word as something with a similar sound and spelling, such as if a student misreads *faith* as *father*. Choices *B* and *C* are examples of syntactic errors (words with similar grammatical functions), while Choice *D* is an example of a semantic error (words with similar meanings).

20. C: Graphemes are the letter(s) that represent phonemes. Phonemes are spoken, while graphemes are written. Graphemes are the letters in the alphabet, but some graphemes may correspond with more than one morpheme (such as the letter *c,* which may produce the /s/ or /k/ sound) and vice versa (the /k/ sound may be represented by the letter *c, k,* or *ck*). Also, a grapheme may be a single letter or more than one letter.

21. A: The best strategy would be to assure him that it's fine to try his best to spell a word how he thinks it sounds. At this stage of spelling, it is expected that students will make errors as they refine their phonological and orthographic skills. Choice *B* is not the best answer because, in fact, the spelling *wud* shows clear phonemic awareness; *would* is an example of a word with uncommon spelling, and *wud* is a logical guess at phonetic spelling. Choice *C* is also not correct because, while formal spelling assessment is important, it does not have to overtake informal in-class assignments. Choice *D* is also incorrect because it does not provide the opportunities for writing practice.

22. B: Teach them as sight words through direct instruction. Students should learn to recognize these common words so they can read them with fluency. Because their spellings do not follow common orthographic rules, it is better for teachers to introduce them through explicit teaching rather than wait for students to learn them implicitly, Choice *A*. Choice *C* is not the best approach for beginner learners, and Choice *D* is also incorrect because some of the most useful high-frequency words are those with irregular spellings.

23. D: *Birthday* ends with an open syllable. An open syllable is one that ends with a vowel sound, while a closed syllable ends with a consonant sound.

24. B: Word families used in building phonemic awareness are those that have the same rime and different onsets. Therefore, *bat, mat, sat* is the correct set.

25. C: A student is able to recognize upper- and lowercase letters as well as the sounds and names of letters. Letter recognition includes not only being able to recite the alphabet but also being able to identify the sounds and the names of letters. Students should also be able to recognize both upper- and lowercase letters in context and in isolation.

26. A: The most appropriate ending digraph sound to learn for a beginning reading class is /sh/ in *bush*. When introducing blends and digraphs, teachers should begin with the most common letter combinations that appear in English. /sh/ is a digraph that students will encounter much more often than the other answer choices.

27. D: She recognized the orthographic pattern *-tion* and understood that words with that ending place stress on the penultimate syllable. When students are able to correctly pronounce multisyllabic words

152

the first time they encounter them, they are relying on their (conscious or unconscious) awareness of syllabication patterns. Choice *A* is not the best answer because simply recognizing a word visually does not always correlate with being able to pronounce it. Choice *B* is also incorrect because, in this case, the affix *-tion* affects the pronunciation of the base words, so simply recognizing those does not account for placing the correct stress in the derived forms. Choice *C* is also not the best answer because, while background knowledge can contribute to vocabulary awareness, it is not the strongest factor in pronunciation knowledge.

Fluency

1. B: Spelling conventions is the area of study that involves mechanics, usage, and sentence formation. Mechanics refers to spelling, punctuation, and capitalization. Usage refers to the use of the various parts of speech within sentences, and sentence formation is the order in which the various words in a sentence appear. Generally speaking, word analysis is the breaking down of words into morphemes and word units in order to arrive at the word's meaning. Morphemes are the smallest units of a written language that carry meaning, and phonics refers to the study of letter-sound relationships.

2. A: Reading fluency involves how accurately a child reads each individual word within a sentence, the speed at which a child reads, and the expression the child applies while reading. Therefore, accuracy, rate, and prosody are the three key areas of reading fluency.

3. A: If a child can accurately read text with consistent speed and appropriate expression while demonstrating comprehension, the child is said to have reading fluency skills. Without the ability to read fluently, a child's reading comprehension, Choice *C*, will be limited.

4. A: The rhythmic sounds and rhyming words of some poems help build a child's phonemic awareness.

5. A: Reading fluency is the ability to accurately read at a socially acceptable pace and with proper expression. Phonetic awareness leads to the proper pronunciation of words and fluency. Once students are able to read fluently, concentration is no longer dedicated toward the process of reading. Instead, students can concentrate on the meaning of a text. Thus, in the developmental process of reading, comprehension follows fluency.

6. B: Strand 11(c) of Competency 11 in the RICA's Content Specifications states the expectation that teachers "(demonstrate the) ability to use the results of assessments to plan effective instruction and interventions ... and adjust instruction and interventions to meet the identified needs of students."

7. D: Word-reading accuracy is often measured by counting the number of errors that occur per 100 words of oral reading. This information is used to select the appropriate level of text for an individual.

8. C: In the babbling stage, children repeat simple syllables that will later form the building blocks of their first words, such as *ma-ma* and *da-da*. Choice *A* is not correct because children learn their first language simply by being exposed to it, without any formal instruction required. Choice *B* is also incorrect because most children utter their first word by about one year old. Babies demonstrate understanding of language before they are able to actually form words themselves, so Choice *D* is not correct.

Vocabulary, Academic Language, and Background Knowledge

1. A: A dialect of a language refers to one version of that language that follows specific patterns of grammar, spelling, pronunciation, and vocabulary. In this sense, then, Standard English is simply one of many different dialects of English. Standard English is not the original form of English because the language has evolved considerably over the past several centuries and will most likely continue to do so in the future. Also, there is nothing that makes Standard English more complex or grammatical than other dialects of English. Although other dialects may deviate from the grammar used in Standard English, these dialects still follow their own predictable rules and patterns of grammar.

2. A: *Slang* refers to non-standard expressions that are not used in elevated speech and writing. *Slang* tends to be specific to one group or time period and is commonly used within groups of young people during their conversations with each other. *Jargon* refers to the language used in a specialized field. The *vernacular* is the native language of a local area, and a *dialect* is one form of a language in a certain region. Thus, Choices *B*, *C*, and *D* are incorrect.

3. D: Colloquial language is that which is used conversationally or informally, in contrast to professional or academic language. While *ain't* is common in conversational English, it is a non-standard expression in academic writing. For college-bound students, high school should introduce them to the expectations of a college classroom, so *B* is not the best answer. Teachers should also avoid placing moral or social value on certain patterns of speech. Rather than teaching students that their familiar speech patterns are bad, teachers should help students learn when and how to use appropriate forms of expression, so Choice *C* is wrong. *Ain't* is in the dictionary, so Choice *A* is incorrect, both in the reason for counseling and in the factual sense.

4. D: The author's word choice that contributes to the style and mood. An author's diction may be elevated, academic, colloquial, melancholy, confessional, or any other mood or way of expression. Discussing a writer's diction requires students to closely consider the types of words used in a text, their denotations and connotations, and the impression they give to the reader.

5. C: Metacognition is another word for "thinking about thinking." By engaging students in this metacognitive activity, the teacher allows students to evaluate their goals, study methods, and strengths and weaknesses, and helps them take responsibility for their own learning process.

6. A: The three most important factors for choosing vocabulary that will contribute the most to students' development are frequency (how often will students encounter this word in their studies?), utility (will students have many chances to use this word in different contexts, or is this word's usage very limited in scope and applicability?), and level of knowledge (is this word already part of students' established vocabulary, or will this word be an opportunity for them to learn something new?).

7. A: Students can get confused with false cognates, hindering comprehension. In language learning, cognates are words in the target language that are similar to words in the student's native language. Particularly for students whose native language shares common roots with English, cognates can aid in learning new vocabulary. However, students may encounter false cognates, or English words that look similar to words in their native language but have different meanings. Choice *D,* in particular, is incorrect because, especially with Latin-based languages, cognates often include academic English vocabulary from Latin roots.

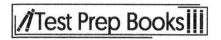

8. C: In selecting academic and content-based texts, teachers should target students' instructional reading level, or the level at which they can understand the text with a small amount of guidance from the teacher; their accuracy level should be between 90 and 94 percent. Frustration reading level, Choice A, refers to the level at which students struggle with the text, have a low level of accuracy and comprehension, and become discouraged about reading. Independent reading level, Choice B, refers to the level at which students can read without any assistance; generally, their accuracy level is 95 percent or higher. Instructional reading level is low enough to still challenge students but high enough that students can comfortably follow the material.

9. B: She wants to activate students' background knowledge on the subject. A KWL chart stands for *know–want to know–learned* and allows students to assess their knowledge before, during, and after a lesson. Beginning a lesson with a KWL chart (the "know" and "want to know" sections) allows students to activate their background knowledge, including key vocabulary and concepts. It is also a way for students to predict and anticipate the text's content. Choice A is incorrect because this is an example of a collaborative activity, not a competitive one. Choice C is also not the best answer because she is trying to engage every student's interest. Finally, Choice D is incorrect because a KWL chart is an informal way for students to explore their ideas about a topic.

10. D: His teacher can give him additional practice in identifying and responding to different question types. Because the student is able to summarize the contents and respond to short-answer questions, it is apparent that he is not struggling with comprehending the text or the topic, so Choices A and C are not the best answers. Rather, he is likely struggling with decoding the different types of academic question forms, such as literal, inferential, and evaluative questions. By building his skills in identifying different question types and patterns, he will be able to more quickly understand what the question is asking and how to locate the information in the text (or whether the question requires him to make an inference not stated in the text, for instance).

11. B: Vocabulary words can generally be divided into Tier 1, Tier 2, and Tier 3. Tier 1 words include high-frequency or sight words, the most basic vocabulary for understanding English. Tier 2 words are more academic words (such as the ones in this example), but they appear across multiple contexts and are not restricted to a single discipline. Finally, Tier 3 words are highly specialized vocabulary related to a single subject (for example, scientific terminology). Tier 4 vocabulary does not exist.

12. B: Students will not have to stop and decode every word and can instead improve their reading rate and focus on overall textual comprehension. Having a strong foundation in sight words (function and high-frequency words) allows students to read those words automatically and instead focus on key content words and decoding any new vocabulary. Choice A is incorrect because, as students progress to higher levels of study, texts will contain fewer sight words and more complex terminology. Choice C is also incorrect because many academic words are based on Greek or Latin roots, not on sight words. Choice D is similarly incorrect; sight words do not prepare students for all the pronunciations they will encounter in developing their academic vocabulary.

13. D: Students are given several examples of *cred* before brainstorming other examples together and are then put in pairs and assigned one new *cred* word to introduce to the class. Reciprocal teaching is based on the gradual release of responsibility model, whereby the teacher introduces a new concept to the class and then gives students the chance to independently engage with the material by making predictions, generating questions, clarifying the content, and summarizing what they have learned.

155

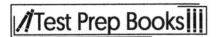

14. B: Synonyms are words whose meanings are the same or similar, such as *happy* and *joyful*. Choice *A* is an example of words that rhyme, Choice *C* is an example of antonyms (words with opposite meanings), and Choice *D* is an example of words with shared roots.

15. C: She should introduce the word through explicit instruction and then give students a chance to read and write the word in context. The most effective vocabulary instruction occurs when words are not introduced in isolation, as in Choice *D*, but when students are given an opportunity to encounter and use words in both classroom and everyday context. Choice *A* is incorrect; studies show that most students can effectively learn up to nine new vocabulary words per week. Choice *B* is also not the best answer because, while it is useful to keep the Word of the Day on the board or on the wall, words should also be reinforced in subsequent lessons that allow students to use what they have learned.

16. B: The students should consider the part of speech and the words closely surrounding the unknown term. Context clues allow readers to guess the meaning of an unfamiliar word by considering the role it plays in a sentence based on semantic and syntactic clues. For example, students can tell that *obsequious* is being used as an adjective, so it is a word that describes a courtier. They can also use the meaning of earlier words they know—in this case, the first sentence's reference to flattery—to guess that an obsequious person is good at flattering others. Choice *A* is not the best answer because context clues are based on information already in the text, not supplementary references. Choice *C* is also not the best answer for a similar reason; context should be based on the text rather than information from other students. Choice *D* is incorrect because prior knowledge is not involved in context clues either.

17. D: Students should learn to recognize the different information contained within a dictionary entry, such as spelling, pronunciation, multiple definitions, and word origins. Dictionaries have a variety of usages beyond just checking spelling. Teachers should explain the different parts of a dictionary entry and allow students to explore things like how to select the most appropriate definition or how the part of speech affects meaning. Choice *A* is not the best answer because, while those are useful decoding skills, students still need to know how and when to access reference materials. Choice *B* is not correct because dictionary skills are relevant for both English Language Learners and native speakers. Finally, Choice *C* is not the best answer; although it is correct, it overlooks many situations in which students may have to choose between more than just the first definition.

18. B: Acquainted words are words that a student has encountered before but is not fully confident using yet. Unknown words, Choice *A*, are those a student has never encountered before; acquainted words are those that are familiar but have not entered regular use in the student's vocabulary; and established words, Choice *D*, are those the student can comfortably use and understand in various contexts.

19. D: Students should be immersed in a language-rich environment where they can explore new words through reading, writing, listening, and speaking. Students should be exposed to language in as many forms as possible to build both academic and real-life language skills. Choices *A* and *C* are not the best answers because speaking and listening are both important aspects of language development in students of all ages. Choice *B* is not the best answer because, while differentiated learning can be helpful, students still need instruction in other modes to continue to develop skills in their weaker areas.

Comprehension

1. B: Both the audience and primary purpose are important for choosing a writing mode. The audience is an important factor as the diction, tone, and stylistic choices of a written piece are tailored to fit the audience demographic. The primary purpose is the reason for writing the piece, so the mode of writing must be tailored to the most effective delivery method for the message. The main idea is the central theme or topic of the piece, which can be expressed in any form the author chooses. Because the mode depends on the reason the author wrote the piece, the main idea is not an important factor in determining which mode of writing to use.

2. C: The main idea of a piece is its central theme or subject and what the author wants readers to know or understand after they read. Choice *A* is incorrect because the primary purpose is the reason that a piece was written, and while the main idea is an important part of the primary purpose, the above elements are not developed with that intent. Choice *B* is incorrect because while the plot refers to the events that occur in a narrative, organization, tone, and supporting details are not used only to develop plot. Choice *D* is incorrect because characterization is the description of a person.

3. A: The passage describes a situation and then explains the causes that led to it. Also, it utilizes cause and effect signal words, such as *reasons*, *factors*, *so*, and *as a result*. Choice *B* is incorrect because a compare and contrast order considers the similarities and differences of two or more things. Choice *C* is incorrect because spatial order describes where things are located in relation to each other. Finally, Choice *D* is incorrect because time order describes when things occurred chronologically.

4. B: Children and less educated audiences tend to understand short, succinct sentences more effectively than longer, complex sentences because short sentences help increase information processing. Choice *A* is incorrect as longer, more fluid sentences are best used for adults and more educated audiences because they minimize processing times and allow for more information to be conveyed. Choices *C* and *D* are incorrect because there is no correlation between a given profession and a writing style; rather, it depends on how familiar the audience is with a given subject.

5. A: The revising stage involves adding, removing, and rearranging sections of a written work. Choice *B* is incorrect as the publishing stage involves the distribution of the finished product to the publisher, teacher, or reader. Choice *C* is incorrect because the writing stage is the actual act of writing the work, and generally does not including editing or revision. Choice *D* is incorrect as the pre-writing stage involves the planning, drafting, and researching of the intended piece.

6. C: Literary analysis of a fictional text involves several areas of study, including character development, setting, and plot. Although point of view refers to a specific area of study in literary analysis, it is only one area. Word analysis does not involve the study of elements within a fictional text.

7. D: Informational texts generally contain five key elements in order to be considered informative. These five elements include the author's purpose, the major ideas, supporting details, visual aids, and key vocabulary. Narratives are accounts—either spoken or written—of an event or a story. Persuasive texts, such as advertisements, use persuasive language to try to convince the reader to act or feel a certain way. Informational texts strive to share factual information about a given subject in order to advance a reader's knowledge.

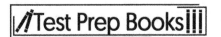

8. A: When a person infers something, he or she is demonstrating the ability to extract key information and make logical assumptions based on that information. The information provided is not direct, but implied. Being able to navigate a variety of texts independently has nothing to do with inference; it demonstrates a student's reading comprehension and fluency. Successfully summarizing and paraphrasing texts are advanced literacy skills that demonstrate a student's reading comprehension and writing proficiency.

9. D: Story maps are a specific type of visual aid that helps younger children develop a clearer understanding of a story being read. Story maps may represent the beginning, middle, and ending of a story, or they may be used to develop a clearer picture of each character's personality and traits, unfold the story's plot, or establish the setting.

10. C: Informational texts organized with headings, subheadings, sidebars, hyperlinks, and other features help strengthen the reader's reading comprehension and vocabulary knowledge. A glossary defines terms and words used within a text.

11. C: Third person is a term used to refer to a specific point of view in literature. A third person omniscient point of view develops the point of view of each character within a given story and allows the reader to understand each character's feelings as well as their interpretation of a story's events. Third person limited only offers insight into one character, usually the main character.

12. B: Narratives are personal accounts of a time period, event, or an individual, with the purpose of documenting, recording, or sharing such factual information. By contrast, fiction is a genre of writing that is fabricated. Informational texts are academic texts used to further a student's mastery of a given subject. Research papers are reports that students research and write to demonstrate their understanding of an area of study.

13. C: Pathos refers to the author's appeal to the audience's or reader's emotions. *Ethos* refers to the level of credibility of a piece of writing. *Logos* refers to the author's appeal to the audience's or reader's logic. *Kairos* refers to the most opportune moment to do something. Therefore, the correct answer is *pathos.*

14. A: Firsthand accounts are given by primary sources—individuals who provide personal or expert accounts of an event, subject matter, time period, or individual. They are viewed more as objective accounts than subjective. Secondary sources are accounts given by an individual or group of individuals who were not physically present at the event or who did not have firsthand knowledge of an individual or time period. Secondary sources are sources that have used research in order to create a written work. Direct sources and indirect sources are not standard terms.

15. C: When authors use hyperbole, they are using extreme exaggeration to strongly state a point or evoke a specific emotion in the reader. Idioms can be in the form of words, phrases, or sentences that are expressed figuratively, but they carry a literal meaning that readers must infer. Metaphors are literary devices that compare two unlike entities, as in "The United States is a melting pot." Alliteration is a poetic device that repeats the beginning consonant sound throughout a sentence or phrase strictly for entertainment—"The **b**all **b**ounced along the **b**lue **b**alcony."

16. D: Flashback is a technique used to give more background information in a story. None of the other concepts are directly related to going back in time.

158

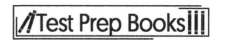

Planning, Organizing, and Managing Reading Instruction Based on Ongoing Assessment

1. A: When students have phonetic problems, instructors should introduce activities that help the students sound out words and analyze their different aspects to build familiarity with English vocabulary and structure. The other choices would be more appropriate activities to aid reading comprehension.

2. C: Percentile scores provide a means of score comparisons and range from 1 to 99. A student's percentile score indicates the percentage of total test takers that student outperformed. For example, a student who scored in the 77th percentile achieved a score that is higher than 77 percent of the rest of the test cohort. A student's percentile score is different than the percentage of correct responses obtained on the test. A percentile score simply compares one student's score with the scores of all of the other students who took the test.

3. D: Interest-based differentiation is based on the concept that students' performance can be associated with their interest level in the subject or activity. Choices *A, B*, and *C* are based on performance or skill level, while Choice *D* is an example of interest-based differentiation. Instructors can encourage reading growth by allowing students to choose their learning activities. Students more interested in auditory activities may find listening to oral reading exercises more engaging than reading alone in their own head.

4. D: Differentiated instruction demands that teachers find ways to allow students to work at their own reading level as they make progress to their reading goals. Therefore, Choice *D* is correct. Choice *A* is incorrect because it confuses differentiated instruction with individualized instruction. Choice *B* is incorrect because it assumes differentiated instruction prioritizes preference over reading level. Choice *C* is incorrect because differentiated instruction relies on small group instruction.

5. A: Choice *A* is correct because only students with a thorough understanding of a written text will be able to make inferences about what they read. Choices *B* and *D* are incorrect because they have more to do with memory than comprehension. Choice *C* is incorrect because whether or not a student writes grammatically correct responses is irrelevant when assessing engagement and comprehension.

6. B: Choice *B* is correct because teachers engage students at varying reading levels by organizing units around a larger context, topic, or theme. Choice *A* is incorrect because exposure to multiple books at varying reading levels is necessary to influence engagement. Choice *C* is incorrect because reader impressions may have little support in the text itself, which is why the best close reading strategies focus on what the text says. Choice *D* is incorrect because the best way to engage students is to assign them with texts at their reading level. Assigning the same texts to everyone in the class may bore advanced readers and discourage those who are further behind.

7. B: The activation of prior knowledge, construction of prerequisite knowledge, commitment to intentional practice, and intermittent introduction of more complex reading material are all part of the scaffolding process, making Choice *B* correct. Choice *A* is incorrect because modeling is the process of demonstrating reading practices. Choice *C* is incorrect because individualized instruction is the practice of curating a curriculum to an individual student's reading goals. Choice *D* is incorrect because differentiated instruction is the process of organizing coursework and assignments around the varying needs of an entire class.

159

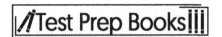

8. C: Choice *C* is correct because, through modeling, teachers verbalize the ways they think about and interact with a text. This demonstrates good reading practices and provides a tangible example for students to model their own reading processes after. Modeling provides students with concrete examples on how to read well. Choice *A* is incorrect because teachers do not use modeling to tell students what or how to think. Choice *B* is incorrect because modeling is not relevant to the creation of a safe reading environment. Choice *D* is incorrect because modeling is not about memorization of text.

9. C: Choice *C* is correct because reading coaches and classroom teachers collaborate on reading curriculum, and they reinforce reading strategies with their students, both inside and outside the classroom. Choice *A* is incorrect because reading coaches are not the only curriculum developers; instead, they work alongside classroom teachers. Choice *D* is incorrect because reading coaches do not necessarily serve as liaisons; classroom teachers often communicate directly with parents/caretakers themselves. Choice *B* is incorrect because it indicates that reading coaches work with students exclusively after school, but reading coaches play a big role during school hours.

10. C: Choice *C* is correct because teachers use feedback from students' self-assessments to develop individual learning goals; students are encouraged to self-evaluate their abilities and articulate their own reading goals. Teachers use their knowledge of a student's own perceptions and motivations to design individualized objectives and secure pertinent resources. Choice *A* is incorrect because teachers use other reading assessments to extract accurate data about their students' progress. Choice *B* is incorrect because it does not indicate a teacher's intention for assigning a student a self-assessment. Choice *D* is incorrect because student self-assessments do not directly reduce student distractions.

11. B: Choice *B* is correct because the zone of proximal development (ZPD) refers to concepts that a student is not yet capable of understanding independently but could understand with guidance from an instructor. Teachers help students tackle concepts within their ZPD by assigning reading material and organizing instruction that facilitates both the mastery of old skills/knowledge and the acquisition of new skills/knowledge. Choice *A* is incorrect because students work with both learned and unlearned material within their ZPD. Choice *C* is incorrect because continued practice with former material should prevent the same mistakes from occurring. Choice *D* is incorrect because the ZPD is an individual metric that does not refer to class average.

12. A: Choice *A* is correct because assessment data equips teachers with information about their students' current reading levels; teachers use this data to decide which types of interventions are necessary. Assessment data enables teachers to develop and implement scaffolding strategies that help students work with more complicated texts. Choice *B* is incorrect because it implies that teachers focus on maintaining a student's current level of reading instruction. Choice *C* is incorrect because helping individual students progress has little to do with organizing instruction around the average reading level of the class. Choice *D* is incorrect because, while assessment data could be compiled into reports, reading assessments should primarily be used to improve instruction and help students progress.

13. B: Choice *B* is correct because scaffolding refers to the temporary supports that teachers and reading coaches use to help students advance to higher reading levels. Temporary supports include decoding strategies and reading aloud, which help a student engage with more complex and challenging texts. Choices *A*, *C*, and *D* do not provide definitions of scaffolding.

14. B: Choice *B* is correct because, through differentiated instruction, teachers employ various methods to evaluate reading comprehension. Based on need and ability, teachers will assign different tasks to

160

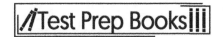

each group. This allows instructors to teach an entire class while varying assessment methods to match the needs of all students. Choice *A* is incorrect because individualized instruction refers to curriculum designed for individual students, usually struggling students, rather than to groups of students with similar reading goals. Choice *C* is incorrect because direct instruction is explicit instruction of a concept, usually in the form of a lecture or lesson given to the entire class. Choice *D* is incorrect because, like direct instruction, whole-class instruction involves the entire class in one lesson or activity.

15. A: Choice *A* is correct because reading interventions should be offered as soon as it is apparent that a student is falling behind. Choice *B* is incorrect because it is normal and expected for students to struggle with difficult material when reading independently; struggles with material at their current reading level are more of a cause for concern. Choice *C* is incorrect because support systems, like parents and caretakers, may be unaware when a student is struggling with reading material, or may request special treatment for their child even when such interventions would be unnecessary. Choice *D* is incorrect because even the best readers will make mistakes; more than one mistake per session is not an automatic indicator of the need for intervention.

16. D: Choice *D* is correct because student learning is not often accelerated by whole-group instruction. During whole-group instruction, teachers go through grade-level material and provide important lessons on reading comprehension and phonics. Learning is accelerated in small groups, where instruction is differentiated and specific to the needs and abilities of individual students. Choices *A*, *B*, and *C* are incorrect because they indicate appropriate reading instruction practices.

17. D: Choice *D* is correct because teachers gain valuable information about student deficiencies in particular skill areas, like phonics and comprehension, from diagnostic assessments. Teachers use this information to organize small groups and develop differentiated and individualized curricula for struggling students. Choice *A* is incorrect because outcomes assessments measure the effectiveness of a reading test overall. Choice *B* is incorrect because screening assessments are assigned at the beginning of a school year to evaluate students identified as high-risk to fall behind. Choice *C* is incorrect because progress monitoring assessments are done either weekly or biweekly to measure a student's progress throughout a reading program.

18. A: Choice *A* is correct because fluency assessments measure a student's ability to recognize and pronounce words correctly within a larger passage. Choice *B* is incorrect because it describes decoding assessments, which measure a student's ability to recognize words on their own. Choice *C* is incorrect because it describes a fluency assessment. Choice *D* is incorrect because it describes a comprehension assessment.

19. D: Choice *D* is correct because literacy-rich environments expose students to ample and diverse sources of reading material, including chapter books, magazines, and non-fiction. Additionally, literacy-rich environments include literacy posters and word walls. Displaying exemplary samples of student work is another great way to promote literacy. Choices *A* and *C* are incorrect because neither describes a method of directly fostering a literacy-rich classroom environment. They contribute more to a student's support system than the environment of the classroom itself. Choice *B* is incorrect because literacy-rich environments start with the promotion of reading material and paraphernalia.

20. A: Choice *A* is correct because substituting one word in a passage for another word that makes sense in context is a good example of a meaning-based mistake. Developing readers occasionally interject words that would fit the context but don't appear in the text. Choice *B* is incorrect because it is an

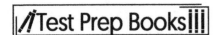

example of a syntactic mistake. Choice *C* is incorrect because it is an example of a phonetic mistake. Choice *D* is incorrect because it is an example of a comprehension mistake.

21. B: Choice *B* is correct because teachers use reading assessments as diagnostic tools. Based on the results of reading assessments, teachers decide what skills each student should focus on, and teachers can organize students into groups based on their current needs and skill levels. Additionally, reading material is assigned to students based on current needs. Choice *A* is incorrect because teachers do not use reading assessments primarily to assign grades; they use reading assessments to measure progress and plan future instruction. Choice *C* is incorrect because IEPs indicate one method of providing specialized instruction, and IEPs may be assigned based on reading assessment, but they do not indicate the reason for reading assessments. Choice *D* is incorrect because it demonstrates how reading assessments are utilized in practice, not why they are assigned.

22. C: Choice *C* is correct because students reading at their frustration reading level make more than one mistake per ten words. Choice *A* is incorrect because students reading at their instructional reading level make no more than one mistake per ten words. Choice *B* is incorrect because students reading at their independent level make no more than one mistake per twenty words. Choice *D* is incorrect because *emergent* is not a term used to describe reading level.

23. D: Choice *D* is correct because students should work with both new and unfamiliar words. Choice *A* is incorrect because building confidence with familiar words should not be the exclusive focus of reading practice. Choice *B* is incorrect because a student who only encounters challenging words is not practicing useful skills at comfortable reading levels. Choice *C* is incorrect because students should move on from current reading levels when they are ready; they should not be inhibited by rigid time frames.

24. D: Choice *D* is correct because valuable information about the areas a child struggles with may become apparent by comparing assessment results with classwork. When reading assessment scores vary from classwork scores to that point, teachers should evaluate the discrepancy with parents. Often, subskills are to blame for lower overall scores. A student who generally does well with reading may struggle with vocabulary or comprehension, so this should be addressed with parents. Choices *A*, *B*, and *C* indicate areas teachers should cover with parents during assessment results meetings.

25. C: Choice *C* is correct because teachers typically administer progress monitoring assessments to students who are identified as at-risk for reading difficulties once a week or every other week. These short assessments measure the efficacy of additional support and intervention strategies. This data allows teachers to make changes to a student's curriculum if necessary. Choices *A*, *B*, and *D* are incorrect because progress monitoring assessments assigned at these intervals would not be completed often enough for intervention strategies to be implemented effectively.

Dear RICA Test Taker,

We would like to start by thanking you for purchasing this study guide for your RICA exam. We hope that we exceeded your expectations.

Our goal in creating this study guide was to cover all of the topics that you will see on the test. We also strove to make our practice questions as similar as possible to what you will encounter on test day. With that being said, if you found something that you feel was not up to your standards, please send us an email and let us know.

We have study guides in a wide variety of fields. If you're interested in one, try searching for it on Amazon or send us an email.

Thanks Again and Happy Testing!
Product Development Team
info@studyguideteam.com

FREE Test Taking Tips DVD Offer

To help us better serve you, we have developed a Test Taking Tips DVD that we would like to give you for FREE. **This DVD covers world-class test taking tips that you can use to be even more successful when you are taking your test.**

All that we ask is that you email us your feedback about your study guide. Please let us know what you thought about it – whether that is good, bad or indifferent.

To get your **FREE Test Taking Tips DVD**, email freedvd@studyguideteam.com with "FREE DVD" in the subject line and the following information in the body of the email:

     a. The title of your study guide.

     b. Your product rating on a scale of 1-5, with 5 being the highest rating.

     c. Your feedback about the study guide. What did you think of it?

     d. Your full name and shipping address to send your free DVD.

If you have any questions or concerns, please don't hesitate to contact us at freedvd@studyguideteam.com.

Thanks again!

Made in the USA
Las Vegas, NV
18 January 2024

84379740R00096